THE TWO ST. JOHNS

OF

THE NEW TESTAMENT.

BY

JAMES STALKER, D. D.,

AUTHOR OF "IMAGO CHRISTI," "THE LIFE OF ST. PAUL," ETC.

> "IN DEVOTIONAL PICTURES WE OFTEN SEE ST. JOHN THE EVANGELIST AND ST. JOHN THE BAPTIST STANDING TOGETHER, ONE ON EACH SIDE OF CHRIST."

WIPF & STOCK · Eugene, Oregon

Wipf and Stock Publishers
199 W 8th Ave, Suite 3
Eugene, OR 97401

The Two St. Johns of the New Testament
By Stalker, James
ISBN 13: 978-1-55635-750-3
ISBN 10: 1-55635-750-8
Publication date 12/3/2007
Previously published by American Tract Society, 1895

Contents.

ST. JOHN THE APOSTLE.

The Disciple Whom Jesus Loved ....PAGE	9
His First Meeting with Christ	23
St. John at Home....................	37
St. John the Apostle	51
St. John One of Three....................	65
St. John's Besetting Sin	79
The Disciple Who Loved Jesus	95
St. John and the Resurrection	109
St. John at Home Again	123
St. John in the Pentecostal Age	141
St. John in Patmos....................	155
The Writings of St. John....................	169

ST. JOHN THE BAPTIST.

I. Birth and Upbringing	189
II. The Prophet	202
III. The Baptism of Jesus	213
IV. His Testimony to Christ....................	224
V. The Eclipse of his Faith....................	236
VI. His Eulogy....................	247
VII. His Martyrdom	259

ST. JOHN THE APOSTLE.

THE
DISCIPLE WHOM JESUS LOVED.

I.

THE aureole round the head of St. John is that he was "the disciple whom Jesus loved." This statement about him is made several times; and in different places both the Greek words for "loved" are employed—both the colder, which expresses esteem, and the more heartfelt, which denotes feeling more tender. As among the patriarchs Abrāham was "the friend of God," and among the kings David was "the man after God's own heart," and among the prophets Dāniel was the "man greatly beloved," so among the followers of the Son of God, during his earthly ministry, St. John was the foremost friend.

We cannot help asking to what he owed this prominence.

Perhaps something was due to an extremely natural cause: it would appear that St. John was, according to the flesh, a cousin of Jesus. The way in which this is made out is as follows: In describing the crucifixion St. Matthew mentions three holy women as witnesses of the tragic scene—Mary Magdalene, Mary the mother of

James and Joses, and the mother of Zebedee's children; St. Mark also mentions three—Mary Magdalene, Mary the mother of James the Less and Joses, and Salome. In St. John four names occur; the first place is given to the Virgin Mary; but the other three are Mary Magdalene, Mary the wife of Cleophas (whom we know from other passages as the father of James and Joses), and Christ's mother's sister. Thus, leaving the Virgin aside, we find two places in each of the three lists occupied by the same two women; but she who occupies the remaining place is called by St. Matthew the mother of Zebedee's children, by St. Mark Salome, and by St. John the sister of the mother of Jesus. It is inferred that she who is designated in these three ways is the same person: her own name was Salome; she was the wife of Zebedee; and she was the sister of the mother of Jesus. If this inference be correct, of course it follows that she was the aunt of Jesus, and that her son John and Jesus were full cousins.

Such a relationship would not have necessarily made Jesus and John friends in the sense indicated by calling John the disciple whom Jesus loved. It might have had precisely the opposite effect. Mary's own sons, the brothers of Jesus, were not, during his lifetime, believers; and there can be little doubt that their very familiarity with him was an obstacle to faith. They could not believe that one to whom they were so closely related was so much greater than themselves. They had seen him so long engaged in the little details of rural existence that it was an offence to their minds when, rising from their narrow lot, he made known his great aims and claims. Not till he appeared to one of them alive after his passion was their unbelief overcome. John might have been affected in the same way by his kinship with Jesus. But, when he escaped this temptation, the natural relationship may have become a bond even within the realm of grace. It was as his Saviour that John loved Jesus; but this may not have prevented him from feeling a peculiarly cordial interest in the affairs of Christ because he was his cousin; and while Christ loved John from the height of his divinity, this may not have prevented him from being drawn to him, and made familiar and confidential, by the operation of the tie of nature.

Cousinship has in multitudes of cases given rise to delightful and helpful associations. There is, indeed, a form of philosophy which scoffs at the obligations created by such relationships. The other day a prominent and educated Socialist asked in public why he should have more to do with his own brother, if he bored him, than with any other man, if he was a good fellow. But nature is not thus to be turned out of doors; human nature, also, is wiser; and Christianity, while not deifying natural relationships, as some religions have done, honors and hallows them. Never were all the beautiful and useful possibilities of cousinship so demonstrated as when Jesus admitted John to the position of the disciple whom he loved.

II.

ALTHOUGH the influence of a natural relationship may have entered into the Saviour's predilection for this disciple, this circumstance could have had no weight at all unless there had been in St. John qualities to support the claim of kinship. But he was one formed by nature to be loved.

If his mother really was the sister of Mary, this points to hereditary advantages enjoyed by St. John. Without having any sympathy with such a doctrine as the Immaculate Conception, we cannot help believing that she who was chosen from among all the daughters of Eve to be the mother of the Perfect Man was, both in mind and body, a rare specimen of womanhood—pure, gentle and gracious. Although her estate was lowly, the blood of kings was in her veins, and in her mind and manners there worked the subtle influence of long descent. Now, what Mary was, it is natural to suppose her sister also was in her own degree; and she was able to impart hereditary advantages to her son.

Certainly there are some of the children of men who appear to be formed of finer clay than their neighbors and cast in a gentler mould. Not infrequently their superiority is stamped even on the outward man, their faces carrying a certificate of excellence which predisposes all who see them in their favor. They are marked out for love; and, if they bear their honors meekly, and if the inward disposition corresponds with the outward promise, they do not as a rule miss the enviable destiny for which nature has intended them. The religious painters of all ages, with whom St. John has always been a favorite subject, have been unanimous in representing him as one of this type. Mrs. Jameson, in her "Sacred and Legendary Art," says, "St. John, in Western art, is always young or in the prime of life, with little or no beard, with flowing or curling hair, generally of a pale brown or golden hue, to express the delicacy of his nature, and in his countenance an expression of dignity and candor." How far in detail the actual St. John may have answered to this description it is of course impossible to say, but there can be but little doubt that the underlying idea is correct.

His must have been a fine and a gifted nature. He was especially strong in the region of the affections—profoundly loving and sympathetic; the heart of Jesus could not have gone out so cordially to him unless it had met with a corresponding return. Yet it is a mistake to think of John's nature as a mere pulp of softness and toleration. There are clear indications, both in the incidents of his life and in his writings, that there burned in him great moral intensity, and that he was capable of strong moral indignation. To speak in the language of philosophy, he was not of the lethargic temperament, but of the melancholic. This is the temperament which beneath an outward demeanor somewhat resembling lethargy conceals the surest and swiftest insight; it keeps silence and broods, but its fire-is only suppressed; it is the temperament which the ancients attributed to their greatest men—to a Sophocles and a Plato, to the philosopher, the poet, the genius.

St. John's writings are before us to show what he was as a thinker, and they thoroughly bear out this estimate. No doubt they are inspired, and the glory in them is due to the Spirit of God; but inspiration did not overlook or override the individuality of the human agents whom it employed, but made use of it, allowing them to speak with their own accent and to think in accordance with the peculiarities of their minds. Now of all the New Testament writers St. John is the most peculiar. He cannot make a remark, or describe a scene, or report a conversation or a speech, without doing it as no one else could. His peculiarity has been described by calling him a mystic: he does not deal much with the outsides of things, but lays hold of everything from within. A scene or occurrence is only interesting to him on account of the idea which it embodies. His thinking is intuitive: he does not reason like St. Paul, or exhort like St. Peter, but concentrates his vision on the object, which opens to his steady gaze. His ideas are not chains of argument, united link to link, but like stars shining out from a background of darkness. He often appears to speak with the simplicity of a child, but under the simple form are concealed thoughts which wander through eternity. Although the materials for writing the life of St. John are meagre, yet no other figure of the New Testament—not even St. Paul or St. Peter—

makes such a distinct impression on the mind of every reader. This is due to his marvellous originality; and it is easy to conceive what a satisfaction it must have been to Christ to have in the circle of his followers one in whom the profundities of his doctrine and the finer shades of his sentiments were sure of sympathetic appreciation.

III.

In spite of these natural advantages and graces, it is true in the fullest sense that St. John was made by Christ. That which the Saviour loved in him was produced by Himself; and here we come upon the deepest reason of the attachment between them. Perhaps no one whom Jesus ever met so much resembled him in natural configuration; but Jesus brought out all that was best in John, and repressed or destroyed what was evil. He imparted himself to his disciple, who did not thereby become less himself, but grew to be what he could never have been without this influence. The loving nature of the disciple found in Christ an excellence on which it could lavish all its affection. In the sayings of Christ his mind obtained truths on which it could brood for ever, finding beneath every depth a deeper still. The supreme characteristic of St. John's thinking is that Christ himself is its centre and circumference. Face to face he was gazing on the person of Christ, and, while this steady, unaverted look revealed the Saviour, it at the same time transfigured himself.

Remarkable as were John's natural powers, there is no reason to believe that, apart from Christ, he would ever have burst through the obscurity in which the life of a Galilean fisherman was enveloped, or have become an influence in the world. But for the redeeming power of Christ his fine qualities might even have been wasted on sinful excesses, as the powers of genius and the wealth of sympathetic natures have often been. But the Saviour not only developed and sanctified John's character, but made him a power for good: he set him on one of the thrones from which the most regal spirits rule the destinies of the race.

It was not, indeed, vouchsafed to St. John to take such a part as St. Peter in the founding of the church. In the Pentecostal days, when the two were associated, St. Peter was always foremost both in speech and action, St. John taking a secondary and subordinate place. Still less had he the world-conquering instincts and the organizing genius of St. Paul. He had his own share, indeed, in the blessed work of spreading the gospel and founding the church. There is a legend of his later life, not without a considerable air of verisimilitude, which illustrates his evangelistic zeal. Preaching in a certain town near Ephesus he was particularly struck with a young man among his auditors, and, at his departure, specially recommended him to the bishop of the place, who took him home and educated him until he was fit for baptism. But the youth fell into evil courses, renounced his profession, and at last went so far as to become the captain of a band of robbers. Subsequently visiting the same town, St. John approached the bishop and asked, "Where is the pledge entrusted to you by Christ and me?" At first the bishop did not understand, but when he remembered he replied, "He is dead—dead to God," and told the sad story of backsliding. Immediately procuring a horse, the apostle set off for the robber's stronghold. He was captured by one of the band and brought before the captain, who, recognizing who his prisoner was, attempted to flee. But the apostle detained him by entreaties, reasoned with him, prayed with him, and never rested till the prodigal returned to the bosom of the church, a pattern of penitence.

Of such scenes there may have been many in St. John's career, but, on the whole, while others were converting the world he was a force in reserve. Yet there slumbered in him the possibility and the intention of a priceless service; and he brought it to perfection when, in his gospel, he gave to mankind the final and incomparable portrait of the Son of God.

There are many services. There is that which can be rendered immediately, and there is that which must ripen first for a lifetime. The ardent young disciple, intent on the undertakings of the hour, may hardly believe at all in the Christianity of the thinker, whose slowly matured thoughts will be fertilizing the church for hundreds of years after his zealous critic is forgotten. But the church has need of those who toil in the depths as well as of those who busy themselves on the surface. She needs her Dantes and Miltons as well as her Whitefields and Wesleys; her Augustines and Pascals as well as her Columbuses and Livingstones; she requires not only the fiery energy of St. Peter and the mighty argumentation of St. Paul, but the exquisite feeling and the mystic depth of St. John.

IV.

It was a special mark of the Lord's affection for St. John that he suffered him to live to a great age. This he indicated himself, when he said to St. Peter, "If I will that he tarry till I come, what is that to thee?" At the beginning St. John appears to have been the youngest of the apostolic circle, but at the close of life he survived all the rest. The age at which he died is variously given by tradition from ninety up to a hundred and twenty years.

The grace of this divine appointment is apparent when we recollect that it was in extreme old age that his Gospel was composed; and the same is probably true of his Epistles. These writings were fruit from an old tree; but the tree was not losing its sap; on the contrary, the fruit was only then fully ripe; and if the tree had been cut down earlier its fruit would never have been gathered.

Besides, the disposition and character of St. John were of a type which shows to great advantage in old age. There are natures to which the gay poet's words apply,

> "That age is best which is the first,
> When youth and blood are warmer;
> But, being spent, the worse and worst
> Times still succeed the former."

There are even types of religious character of which this is true: it is best to see them when their zeal is new and their speculation fresh: afterwards they appear exhausted, or they harden into dogmatism and censoriousness. But St. John's religion was of the type described by a poet of a different order:

> "And in old age, when others fade,
> Their fruit still forth shall bring,
> They shall be fat and full of sap,
> And aye be flourishing."

His later life is surrounded with a halo of legends, which unite in conveying the impression that his old age was exquisitely beautiful. Thus, it is told that he used to keep a tame partridge; and one day a noble huntsman, coming upon him as he was fondling it, expressed surprise that a man of such renown and unworldliness should be so trivially engaged. But the saint answered him, "Why is it that you do not carry the bow in your hand always bent?" And when the huntsman answered, "Because then it would lose its elasticity." "So," rejoined the saint, "do I relax my mind with what appears to you a trivial amusement, that it may have more spring and freshness when I apply it to divine mysteries." Everyone knows the legend of how, when too old and weak to walk, he used to be carried into the Christian assembly and, when seated in the teacher's chair, to utter only the words, "Little children, love one another;" and how, when they asked him why he always repeated this precept, he said, "Because, if you have learned to love, you need nothing more." A legend also obtained currency, that, being of priestly descent, he wore on his brow in old age the petalon of the high priest, that is, the golden plate, fastened on a blue band, with the inscription, "Holiness to the Lord." But obviously this is only a mythical expression for the impression produced by the priestlike dignity and the beauty of holiness with which his old age was encompassed. Indeed, the fragrance of love, truth and sanctity which breathed from this life in its later stages lingered in the atmosphere of the early Church for generations.

Some have regarded this late development of St. John's influence as a prophecy. St. Peter first stamped himself on the Church, then St. Paul, last St. John. And, as it was in that first period of Christianity, so was it to be in the subsequent ages. For fourteen centuries St. Peter ruled Christendom, as was symbolized by the church inscribed with his name in the city which was, for most of that period, the centre of the Christian world; then, at the Reformation, St. Paul's influence took the place of St. Peter's, St. Paul's doctrines being the soul of Protestantism. But the turn of St. John has still to come: his spirit will dominate the millennial age. Perhaps in the individual Christian three such stages may also be distinguished — the period of zeal to begin with, when we resemble St. Peter; the period of steady work and reasoned conviction, when we follow in the steps of St. Paul; the period of tolerance and love, when we are acquiring the spirit of St. John. But we will not defer to any distant stage of life the imitation of the apostle of love. "Now abideth faith, hope, charity, these three; but the greatest of these is charity." "Love is the fulfilling of the law ;" and it is the fulfilment of life; it is both the perfection and the blessedness of humanity. But where shall it be found? what is its secret? St. John, who knew, has told us : it springs from faith in him who is love, and in the work which love led him to do on our behalf: " We love him, because he first loved us."

HIS FIRST MEETING WITH CHRIST.

V.

CONTACT with Christ was not the beginning of the religious experience of St. John. He had been caught in another religious movement before he was connected with that of which Christ was the centre. He was a disciple of the Baptist before becoming a disciple of Christ.

At the close of many barren generations, during which prophecy had been dumb and spiritual death had brooded over the land, suddenly, in the valley of the Jordan, a voice was raised in which the authentic thunder of inspiration was clearly discernible : and simultaneously the Wind of God began to move and murmur in every part of the land. Noteworthy it is how any voice or movement in which the Divine actually announces itself stirs the sleeping instincts of humanity ; for man is made for God, and, however dead his religious nature may appear to be, it is only slumbering : let the right summons be heard and it will respond. The rumor of the Baptist's preaching quickly spread from Dan to Beersheba; and in susceptible souls it awakened curiosity and longing. It drew the shepherd from the hill, the husbandman from the vineyard, the fisherman from his boats, and even the rabbi from his books. Its influence was especially potent over young men; and in the crowds which soon thronged the banks of the river where John baptized were the brightest and most promising spirits of the nation.

Among these was St. John, attracted southward from his occupation on the Sea of Galilee. And he was not only one of the Baptist's hearers but one of his disciples. The first time we see him he is closely attached to the Baptist's person: "John stood, and two of his disciples," one of whom was Andrew and the other John. This shows that the movement had had free course in his spirit: he had taken in the Baptist's message, submitted to the baptismal rite, and, instead of at once returning home, remained to profit by his instruction.

Two things this experience must have done for the future apostle. The Baptist's preaching consisted of two principal parts: first, the message of repentance, and, secondly, the announcement that the kingdom of God was at hand.

St. John, then, had repented. The sense of guilt had been awakened in him, and he had felt the pain and shame of being self-condemned and God-condemned. What the particular sins may have been which had marred his early life and now rose up to trouble his conscience we cannot tell. It is easy to conceive the profanity and recklessness on which St. Peter, in the same circumstances, had to look back; but one would suppose that the boyhood and youth of St. John had been singularly free from anything gross or regrettable. The sense of sin is not, however, proportionate to the magnitude of guilt. While the worst sinners are often utterly insensible to their own spiritual deformity, the whitest souls are sensitively aware of their own shortcomings. There is no human life, either in youth or age, so perfect but that, when enlightened by the Spirit of God, it will see itself to be altogether as an unclean thing.

This experience exerted on St. John a lifelong influence. He became the apostle of love, and it is to him more than anyone else that the world owes the doctrine that God is love; but, unlike some teachers, who, starting from this position, have represented God as so loving that He overlooks the guilt of erring human beings, St. John combines the doctrine of love with the profoundest and even sternest views in regard to the sinfulness of humanity and the need of penitence and atonement. Shallow views in theology are generally due to slight personal experience of repentance. But St. John went through the school of the Baptist to the school of Christ; and the deepest Christian spirits have followed the same pathway.

The other element in the Baptist's message was no less influential. He proclaimed that the kingdom of God was at hand. This was the revival of the hope which had stirred the godly and the patriotic in Israel for hundreds of years—the hope of the reign of God in the land and in the world, which meant at the same time the reign of righteousness and peace. This lifted St. John and the other disciples of the Baptist out of themselves, to take an interest in the weal of their country and the welfare of humanity. To a youthful mind nothing is so good as the awakening of unselfish enthusiasm. Childhood is ensheathed in an unconscious and natural selfishness; manhood is too often the prey of deliberate selfishness; but in youth everyone who is at all divinely-souled feels stirrings of the desire to live for others and to make the world better. Too often, indeed, these emotions are short-lived: having nothing substantial to feed upon they die away, and selfishness supervenes. But St. John obtained from the Baptist faith in a cause fitted not only to feed enthusiasm but to increase it; for the kingdom of God is an object on which unselfish passion can expend all its resources; and it outlives every individual supporter.

These two experiences go well together and supplement each other. Repentance alone makes the spirit morbid, and, if indulged too exclusively, may degenerate into a form of selfishness. Enthusiasm for the kingdom of God, on the other hand, if unconnected with repentance is apt to become visionary and vainglorious: many are willing to reform the world who need first to be reformed themselves. The true order is that of John's experience: to begin within, with reconciliation to God, and then, with a spirit of union with him, to go forth to the regeneration of humanity.

VI.

How long John was a disciple of the Baptist we cannot tell. But at last he was ripe for further development.

It is the immortal glory of the Baptist that he was fully conscious of the preparatory and subordinate nature of his own mission. His was only a herald's voice announcing the approach of the King. Others attempted to make him a rival of the Messiah; but " he confessed, and denied not, but confessed, I am not the Christ," and added, " He must increase, but I must decrease." Never, however, was this attitude so difficult as when he had to transfer his own disciples to Christ. To have in his company one like St. John must have been an unspeakable satisfaction; but, as he stood with St. John and St. Andrew, he pointed to Jesus passing by and said, " Behold the Lamb of God," thus releasing them from further adherence to himself.

It is generally taken for granted that, of the two elements in the Baptist's message, the second — the coming of the kingdom of God — was at first the one most prominent in the minds of the followers of Jesus: they are supposed to have been drawn to him chiefly by Messianic hopes: but these words appear to indicate that the reverse was the case, and that the first part of John's message—the experience of repentance— was that in which they were chiefly absorbed.

It is, indeed, a question what precisely the Baptist

meant by designating Jesus as "the Lamb of God." A choice passage in an exquisite book derives the name from the imagery of the twenty-third Psalm—that lay of perfect peace—" the most complete picture of happiness that ever was or can be drawn. It represents that state of mind for which all alike sigh, and the want of which makes life a failure to most; it represents that *heaven* which is everywhere if we could but enter it, and yet almost nowhere because so few of us can. The two or three who win it may be called victors in life's conflict; to them belongs the *regnum et diadema tutum*. They may pass obscure lives in humble dwellings, or, like Fra Angelico, in a narrow monastic cell, but they are vexed by no flap of unclean wings about the ceiling. From some such humble dwelling Christ came to receive the prophet's baptism. The Baptist was no lamb of God. He was a wrestler with life; one to whom peace of mind does not come easily, but only after a long struggle. He was among the dogs rather than among the lambs of the Shepherd. He recognized the superiority of Him whose confidence had never been disturbed, whose steadfast peace no agitations of life had ever ruffled. He did obeisance to the royalty of inward happiness." These beautiful words undoubtedly express a truth and afford a genuine glimpse of Jesus and the Baptist on this occasion; but they leave out the words—" who taketh away the sin of the world."

Others have gone back for the derivation of the Baptist's phrase to the fifty-third chapter of Isaiah, especially to the words, "He is brought as a lamb to the slaughter, and, as a sheep before her shearers is dumb, so he openeth not his mouth." This would demonstrate that John had grasped the idea of a suffering Messiah. The opposition which he had met with himself and his observation of the temper of the people, and especially of the ruling classes, had convinced him that the Messiah, instead of being welcomed with open arms, would be opposed and persecuted; thus the sin of the world would concentrate itself on Him, and He would have to endure the consequences.

But more than this must surely be in the name. Whether or not, as others suppose, the Baptist had in his mind the paschal lamb or other lambs of sacrifice, when we remember to whom he was speaking—to his own disciples, who had undergone in his school the discipline of repentance — we cannot but conclude that by the Lamb taking away the sin of the world he intended to point Christ out as one who could deal more effectively with sin than he had been able to do. His own work was preliminary: he aroused the conscience, but he could not satisfy it. What, then, was the next step? What virtue was to be looked for in the Fulfiller who was to come after John? While it would be unhistorical to attribute to the Baptist a developed doctrine of atonement, it is equally to miss the point of the situation not to recognize that the prime recommendation of the Messiah to those whom John was addressing was that he should be *the Saviour from sin*.

VII.

ENCOURAGED by their master, and attracted by the appearance of Christ, the two disciples of the Baptist followed the departing figure of Jesus. Hearing their footsteps behind him, he turned and asked, "What seek ye?" This is the first saying of our Lord recorded by St. John; and some have found in it deep meanings—as if it were an invitation to all to seek from him whatever they desired, and he would satisfy them. But we will content ourselves with something simpler — its consideration and kindness. The two seekers were shy, and afraid to introduce themselves; those at their stage of experience often are. A very little will sometimes turn aside an inquiring spirit. But Jesus met them half-way and put them at their ease. They replied by asking him where he dwelt, evidently intimating that they intended sometime to pay him a visit. But he invited them to an interview at once, saying, "Come and see." This also teaches a lesson: seekers ought to be dealt with without delay, because their impressions are apt to evaporate. Many have intended to visit Christ, putting off, however, till to-morrow; but some form of distraction has come in, and the intention has never been carried into effect.

So Jesus took the young men with him to the lodging in which he was staying, and they abode with him that day. St. John tells us the very hour of the

HIS FIRST MEETING WITH CHRIST. 31

clock when this happened: "it was the tenth hour," which some take to mean ten in the forenoon, others four o'clock in the afternoon. At all events Jesus afforded them a prolonged interview, lasting for hours. The scene, the hour, the duration of their stay, the very looks on the face of Jesus, had all remained in the apostle's memory. Most days in anyone's life are forgotten: they sink out of sight and are indistinguishable from multitudes like them. But some days are ever memorable: we can recollect the very hour of the day when each thing took place; the very tones in which words were uttered, the very gestures with which acts were accompanied. Which days are thus imprinted on the memory? None more than those on which we have made acquaintances and formed connections by which our subsequent life has been powerfully influenced. And among such surely the first acquaintance with Christ may well be a marked date. In one sense, indeed, to remember this is impossible; for our acquaintance with him goes back beyond our earliest memory. But it is one thing to hear about Christ from others, and another actually to come in contact with him, and speak with him face to face. With many, at least, this is a subsequent experience, occurring within the period of conscious memory; and, if such an incident is remembered at all, it is likely to be a vivid and a treasured recollection.

These being such never-to-be-forgotten hours of St. John's experience, we naturally expect to learn from him what was the subject of conversation, and what Jesus said. In this, however, we are entirely disappointed, not a word of detail being given. This is the more surprising because St. John's gospel is distinguished for the frequency with which it narrates private interviews with Jesus. What can be the explanation? It has been suggested that John had forgotten; but this is in a high degree unlikely. A better explanation may be gathered from the other incidents of this remarkable day.

It would appear that the method taken by our Lord to impress himself upon those who were introduced to him at this stage was to make them feel that he had a superhuman insight into their thoughts and their character. Thus he met Simon with the announcement that he was in future to bear the name of Peter. And he met Nathanael with such full information about himself that he who had at first incredulously asked, "Can any good thing come out of Nazareth?" burst out with, "Rabbi, thou art the Son of God, thou art the King of Israel!" Now may we not suppose that to St. John also at this time Jesus gave proof of his supernatural knowledge of his history and his inmost thoughts, communicating perhaps some sweet secret as to his future relation to himself and his kingdom? Such a communication a deep, reticent nature like St. John's might feel to be too sacred for reporting. Scripture seems to give ample encouragement to make religious experiences public when there is an inner impulse to do so; but the impulse not to disclose everything is equally sacred. Some experiences would be profaned by being described; the soul has things of its own with which no stranger intermeddles. Nothing is more valuable to our fellowmen than the communication of genuine religious experience if we are free to tell it; but every soul of any depth and intensity has many secrets which it neither could nor would disclose. And of this nature may have been the first confidence vouchsafed to St. John.

VIII.

Something sealed the lips of the evangelist from telling what took place at this interview; but if we had any doubt as to whether or not the communication was one of supreme importance, or whether the hearts of the two hearers burned within them as they listened to Jesus for the first time, we should be convinced by observing how they acted when they issued from the house. Both hastened away to make their experience known; evidently because they were full of what had happened.

It is only, indeed, in a peculiar way that we learn this about St. John. The narrative says of St. Andrew, "He first findeth his own brother Simon," and tells him. But why "first"? This implies that the other young man also found his own brother and did the same. It is an extreme instance of the reticence and modesty with which in his Gospel St. John refers to himself and his relatives. He never mentions his brother or his mother by name. In the present passage he describes himself only as "another disciple," though there is no doubt to whom he refers. In estimating the character of St. John this reserve should be noticed as a prominent characteristic; and it harmonizes well with the other qualities of his exquisite nature.

Both, then, separating at the door of Jesus' lodging, hastened away to tell; and each went to his own brother. The latter circumstance is surely a touching

HIS FIRST MEETING WITH CHRIST.

and instructive trait. The instinct to bear testimony to religious experience is a natural one; but it does not always lead those who are inspired with it to their own homes. Indeed, the very last persons to whom some would think of speaking on religious topics are their own relatives. It is easier to speak in public, for strangers do not know how far our conduct may be in agreement with our words. To our relatives this is accurately known; but just on this account is it safe and wholesome to begin with them: it is a far stronger pledge to consistency. Besides, it is the dictate of nature; if we have any blessed discovery to reveal, surely those first deserve the benefit of it who are our own flesh and blood.

Andrew and John had a blessed discovery to make known. The word with which they broke in upon their astonished brothers was, "We have found." The same word was used by Philip to Nathanael; and Archbishop Trench has called this the Eureka chapter.

What had they found? "We have found Him of whom Moses, in the law, and the prophets did write"—they had found the fulfilment of the law and of the prophets: of the law, whose unfulfilled commandments had been searching their awakened consciences; of the prophets, whose unfulfilled predictions had inflamed their patriotic hopes. So they expressed the discovery in the language of their time and in accordance with their own experience. But it can be expressed in many forms. There is something which all men need; and consciously or unconsciously all are seeking it. Many know they have not found it; many more are unhappy they know not why, but this is the reason. Some think they have found it, but the discovery turns out to be a deception. Men toil and moil for it; they hasten over seas; they search continent after continent; they tear out the bowels of the earth. What is it? What is it that can make life a success, that can fill the heart, that can afford to desire at once both satisfaction and stimulation, that can supply life with an aim, that can guarantee unending progress, that can fill the immeasurable spaces of eternity? Is there any object which can do all this for man? Andrew and John came out from their interview with Jesus crying, "We have found;" St. John wrote this down at the close of a great and happy life in token that he still believed it; and since then millions upon millions have set to their seal that it is true.

ST. JOHN AT HOME.

IX.

St. John's first meeting with Jesus took place on the banks of the Jordan, where he was in attendance on the services of a religious revival and spending days of leisure among a multitude of strangers; his second decisive meeting with him took place at home, in the midst of his friends and when he was engaged in his ordinary work. On the first occasion he sought Jesus; on the second Jesus came to seek him. This is in accordance with the law and practice of Christ's kingdom: if, on sacred days and in sacred places, where the multitude convene for religious purposes, we seek Jesus and find him, he is quite certain to find us out, subsequently, in our week-day life—in the home and at business—and demand recognition and service in the presence of our ordinary acquaintances.

The home of St. John was on the Séa of Galilee—a charming place in which to be born and brought up; for it was the loveliest spot of a lovely country. On account of the great depth of the basin of the lake, 680 feet below the level of the sea and much more below the tableland of Galilee, it enjoyed a tropical climate; the hills, which sloped down to the water's edge, were covered with the choicest crops; and at their feet were bowers of olive and oleander, or meadows gay with a thousand flowers. In the midst of this wealth of foliage lay the heart-shaped expanse of water like a sapphire set in an emerald, except when storms, sweeping down from the gullies of the neighboring hills, churned it into foam.

The frequency of wind on the lake modified the heat of the climate and rendered an active life more easy; and, therefore, although a scene of tropical beauty, the district was the very reverse of a scene of idleness. The fish in the lake were so extraordinarily numerous that they not only supplied food to the neighborhood, but were sent in large quantities to satisfy the hunger of the multitudes who assembled in Jerusalem at the annual feasts and were even known in distant seaports of the Mediterranean. As more than one of the most frequented highways of the ancient world passed through the basin of the lake, there was also an extensive transport trade, as many as four thousand boats plying for this purpose on its limited surface, which measured only fifteen miles by eight. Subserving these chief industries, others, like boat-building and cooperage, occupied a vast population. Nine towns, with fifteen thousand inhabitants apiece, according to a contemporary witness, surrounded the shore, which at the more populous points must have presented the appearance of a continuous city.

Here, then, amid sights and sounds of beauty to fascinate the heart and occupations to employ the mind, St. John had grown up; and there had been nothing in his youth to suggest that his destiny was to be different from that of the other sons of obscurity and toil who, in that corner of the world, had rejoiced, sorrowed and died from generation to generation. But it is impossible to predict what may be the history of any son of Adam. However humble may be the spot where he is born in time, his spirit comes out of the infinite azure of eternity, and its possibilities are incalculable. Besides, St. John belonged to a nation no child of which was safe from thoughts soaring far beyond its birthplace and its own generation, because he was heir to a splendid past and a still more splendid future. In point of fact, the lake on whose margin St. John was born was destined to be lifted up out of its obscurity into everlasting visibility and renown, and in this splendid destiny he was to participate. But it was the coming of Jesus which made all the difference.

X.

The exact spot in the lake region where St. John was born is not known with certainty. But he informs us himself that "Philip was of Bethsaida, the city of Andrew and Peter;" and, as we learn from the other evangelists that he and his brother James were partners in business with Andrew and Peter, the probability is that they belonged to the same place. Bethsaida has been long ago blotted out of existence, and there is some difficulty in identifying its site; many, indeed, have believed that there existed two towns of this name, one on each side of the Jordan where it enters the lake, but this is improbable. There is no doubt, however, that Bethsaida stood in the opener, busier and more beautiful part of the region.

If it be the case that John and James, as well as Philip, Andrew and Peter, belonged to Bethsaida, the fact emerges, that from this one small town Jesus obtained five out of his twelve apostles—a circumstance only paralleled in its singularity by the opposite fact, that of the twelve not one belonged to Jerusalem. All five had also apparently been disciples of the Baptist before becoming disciples of Jesus. What can have been the explanation of a combination so remarkable? Was there a rabbi in the synagogue of Bethsaida who had trained the youth of the place in piety and aspiration? All the teachers even of that soulless age were not bad men. Or was it to the prayers of their parents

that this galaxy of youthful earnestness was due?
From the fact that Zebedee offered no opposition to
his sons when they left their business to follow Jesus
we may infer that his sympathies were on the right
side. His wife, Salome, appears later as an enthusiastic supporter of the good cause. In Bethsaida there
may have been a circle of godly souls whose united
prayers were answered when their sons simultaneously
joined the religious movements of the Baptist and Jesus.
Or was it one of the young men themselves by whose
magnetism the rest were drawn into the paths of peace?
If so, was this leader John, or Peter, or one of those
less known? One likes to speculate on the possible
causes of such a phenomenon, even though we cannot
hope for a decided answer. Five young men of the
same town could not, all together, have taken such
a course without some powerful influence being at work
in secret. Every visible pillar in the temple of God
rests upon an invisible one sunk beneath the surface of
history. Honor to the unknown workers, who have no
name or fame on earth but without whose labor and
patience the edifice could not have been erected!

Besides John, his father, his brother and his partners, we see in the boats on this occasion "hired servants"; and this circumstance has been combined with
other slight indications in the Gospels to support the
inference that St. John belonged to a condition in life
considerably removed from poverty, with the possibility
of connections even with the more select classes of society. However this may be, he certainly was a young
man well known in the neighborhood to which he be-

longed; and the names and figures mentioned in the narrative easily enable us to summon up before the mind's eye a larger circle of relatives and acquaintances, by whom he was surrounded, when the crisis of his life arrived and he had to make the decisive choice. Their eyes were upon him; their tongues, he could not but be aware, would criticise his action. But Christ, who had obtained his worship before at a distance and among strangers, had now come to summon him to take up the cross of confession and follow him in the place of his abode and in the presence of his neighbors.

XI.

John was at work when Jesus approached him. In the neighboring fields the great Teacher was followed by a vast multitude, to whom he had been preaching. Perhaps the sound of his voice had penetrated to the boat where John was. But the fisherman could not join the congregation, because he was occupied with unavoidable duty. Indeed, he had been at work all night, as fishermen on the Sea of Galilee often were; and he could not leave in disorder the nets which they had been using. So there he was at work, mending the nets, with marks of his prolonged toil visible on his person and his clothes, when Jesus came.

Jesus did not tell him that he ought to have been in the congregation, listening to the Word instead of fishing. On the contrary, he sent him back again to fish. He even entered into partnership with him, telling him the exact spot of the lake to which to go and the side of the ship from which to cast out the net. Thus St. John learned that Christ knew more about the sea than he, though he had lived on it all his days, and he found out how successful work is when in the doing of it the advice of Jesus is followed. We think that it is only with our spiritual affairs that Jesus is concerned, but he knows about our occupation, whatever it may be, better than we do ourselves. Many are afraid that, if they listened to the voice of Jesus when they are at their work, they could not get on; but the experience of St. John proves the very opposite.

Perhaps this experience was intended to convince St. John and his associates that in all their successes on the water in the past a higher Hand had been at work than they had always realized. "Every good and every perfect gift is from above;" whether it come by the direct path of miracle or in more circuitous ways. But the great lesson of the occasion bore upon the future. Jesus was about to call away St. John and his partner from their boats and nets; they were practical men, accustomed to earn their bread and look sharply after their hardly-earned gains; they could not but ask on what they were to depend, and what provision was to be made for those whom they left behind. The miracle of the draught of fishes was the answer to these unexpressed inquiries. Could they doubt the ability to provide of One who so evidently had the resources of nature at his command?

Yet even this was not the profoundest effect which Jesus produced on their spirits. St. Peter, grovelling in the bottom of the boat at the feet of Jesus and crying, "Depart from me, for I am a sinful man, O Lord," gave expression to the sentiment which was in all their hearts, and especially, we may be sure, in the sensitive heart of St. John. In modern arguments about miracles these occurrences are generally spoken of as if they had been irresistible demonstrations addressed to the intellect. This, however, does not appear to have been the way in which they acted. Their effect was moral; they told upon the emotional nature. A miracle happening beside anyone conveyed an overwhelming impression that God was near; and the spectator shrank into himself as a weak and guilty being. Must not the most convincing proof in the religious sphere always be of this nature? As the sun requires no demonstration when we are standing in the light and warmth of his beams, so the best proof of God is his presence and his working. Life does not lack experience of which every unsophisticated mind spontaneously says: "This also cometh forth from the Lord of hosts, who is wonderful in counsel and excellent in working." Nor are these experiences far to seek. As the boat of St. John was transformed into a theatre for the manifestation of Christ's power, so is the pathway of the humblest strewn with experiences which announce the living God; and the Spirit of God strives with every human soul.

XII.

WHEN Christ had subdued the minds of St. John and his companions with an overpowering sense of his authority, he uttered the call for which he had been preparing them. But he couched it in the simplest terms, still keeping to the level of their actual life: "I will make you," he said, "fishers of men."

He was calling them away from the employment by which they had hitherto earned their bread; but they were still to continue to be fishers. Between their past and their future life there was to be no violent break. The skill and experience which they had acquired by faithfulness in the lower sphere were still to be available in the new sphere to which he was calling them up. "All things are double one against another," says the sage of the apocryphal book of Ecclesiasticus; the spiritual and the temporal worlds correspond each to each; and a human being cannot exercise any honest calling conscientiously without learning from it lessons about things on a loftier plane and being prepared for a higher service.

When they afterwards reflected, as they must have done a thousand times, on what it signified to be fishers of men, no better commentary could possibly have been found than Christ's own method on this occasion in dealing with themselves. He was the supreme Fisher, and this day he was fishing for them. He approached them cautiously: they saw the crowd in their vicinity, and this aroused their curiosity before he came near. Then he asked the loan of their boat, to serve for a pulpit; and thus, to a certain extent, they were made partners in his work and interested in its success. Then he showed his interest in their work and astonished them by his knowledge of where the fishes were to be found. Step by step he led them on, till at last the glory of his superiority flashed upon them and they were at his feet, ready to do whatever he might say. This is the way to fish for men—gradually, cautiously, delicately. Weighty above all is the law enunciated by St. Paul, and supremely illustrated on this as on every occasion by Christ—first that which is natural, afterwards that which is spiritual. The fisher for men must find people where they are; he must understand human nature and human life; the more he knows about common occupations the better: he must be able to sympathize with men's reverses and successes, with the subtle movements of womanly feeling, and even with the dreams of childhood; he must believe that God is leading human beings to himself along the pathway of their daily experience, and that it is only as he co-operates with this intention of Providence that he can do them good.

Minor lessons about the art to which they were being called were also to be learned by looking back. They had toiled all night and caught nothing; so it is sometimes the lot of the fisher of men to labor in vain and expend his strength for naught. Again, both the hour and the place in which the Lord told them to fish appeared unpropitious; because the best time for fishing was by night, whereas he sent them to it in daylight; and fish are generally most plentiful inshore, while he sent them forth into the deep. So in spiritual fishing, the most unlikely spots and the most unpromising seasons sometimes yield the best results. And, at all events, whenever we have the Lord's command to launch them forth, there ought to be no hesitation to go and, at his word, let down the nets for a draught. St. John and St. Peter must often have wondered when in the spiritual waters they would see anything corresponding to the take of that morning, when the sea seemed alive with fishes and their nets could not contain them all. But this hope was gloriously fulfilled when, at Pentecost and in the times of refreshing which followed, they saw men by the thousand being brought, through the preaching of the cross and the outpouring of the Spirit, into the net of the Kingdom.

XIII.

Jesus had given the call; it was impressive and it had gone home; but it remained to be seen whether those to whom it had been addressed would respond.

To obey involved a serious practical step. Jesus had said, "Follow me, and I will make you fishers of men." They were not to be fishers of men at once: they were to be made so by degrees, and the art was to be acquired by following him. This is the rule always; this is the only way to learn; none can be fishers of men who have not first followed Jesus.

But for them this implied the forsaking of their homes and the business they had learned, that they might literally accompany him whithersoever he went. This could not be an easy thing. St. Peter was already married, and though St. John probably was not thus bound he was a partner in a business in which his father, growing old, required his strength and skill. Life is a complicated thing, and it is never easy to wrench one's self out of the position in which one has been fixed by time and custom. Doubtless there were neighbors who would consider it an unwise thing to let go a business which might be prosperous in order to go after a wandering rabbi, whose aims and pretensions were problematical. But on the spot they left all—boats, nets, relatives—even the miraculous draught of fishes, apparently, they did not stay to secure; they left all, rose up, and followed him.

For the most of us, to follow Jesus does not involve the quitting of home or the throwing up of business: we are called to follow him at home and in business. Yet it does in every case involve self-denial and sacrifice. He calls us away from excessive and exclusive devotion to any earthly thing, whether it be pleasure or home or business. Many are starving their spiritual life, and declining every invitation to usefulness, because they cannot drag themselves away from the making of money or the engagements of society. Even the hours of the day of rest are denied to God—of course they have no time for worship during the week—and the needs of a perishing world appeal to them in vain. Does it not shame us to read, "They left all, rose up, and followed him"? What have we left? What are we sacrificing? "They were stoned, they were sawn asunder, were slain with the sword, being destitute, afflicted, tormented." Such things have men been able to do and to bear for the sake of religion: they have gladly laid down their lives for Christ. How much are we able to do and to suffer for the same sacred cause?

ST. JOHN THE APOSTLE.

XIV.

There were three stages in St. John's connection with Christ. The first was when he was introduced to Him by the Baptist and, in a private interview on the bank of the Jordan, became convinced that He was the Messiah. This may be called the stage of the Believer. Thereafter John returned to his ordinary calling as a fisherman, till, on the strand of the Sea of Galilee, he was sought out by Jesus and summoned to become his constant follower; and he left all, rose up, and followed him. This may be called the stage of the Disciple. How long this stage lasted we cannot tell with precision, but there was still an attainment to be reached. Jesus was in the height of his popularity, and great numbers of disciples were attaching themselves to him, and following him wherever he went. When from among these he selected twelve, that their connection with him might be more special, the third stage of St. John's progress was reached—the stage of the Apostle.

With these stages of St. John's experience may be compared the history of anyone who is called to the public ministry of the gospel. First, his experience is an entirely private one—a meeting with Jesus for his own salvation—and at this stage he may have no thought of devoting his life exclusively to the service of the gospel; he is merely a believer. By-and-by, however, the impulse to be a preacher overpowers him, and he may have to give up some other calling in order to devote himself to the work of preparation. This may last for years, during which he is a learner or disciple. At last, when his course of preparation is completed, he is solemnly set apart to the work of the ministry in a definite sphere, where he speaks and acts in the name of Christ, and his service should be apostolic.

In the experience of private Christians the analogy may not be so perfect. Yet the broad principle applies to all, that, if we are connected with Christ, our connection with him should constantly be growing closer, and the line of progress is indicated by these three words—Believer, Disciple, Apostle, or their equivalents—Faith, Knowledge, Service.

How important this third stage was in the progress of St. John and the rest who were elevated to the honor of apostleship is shown by the way in which Jesus prepared them, and still more by the way in which he prepared himself for the occasion.

One of the Evangelists introduces his account of the election of the Twelve with these words: "It came to pass in those days that he went out into a mountain to pray, and continued all night in prayer to God; and, when it was day, he called unto him his disciples, and of them he chose twelve, whom he also named apostles." Thus we learn that he prepared himself for this act by a night of prayer. His habit of retiring to solitude for prayer is well known; he would go away for an hour or two after the labor of the day was over, or rise up for this purpose a great while before day; but this is perhaps the only occasion when we read that he spent a whole night in prayer. It shows his sense of the gravity of the step which he was about to take; and what a lesson it is to us as to the manner in which we should approach important decisions in our own lives!

Another of the Evangelists introduces the scene differently. He tells how in those days the crowds attending upon the ministry of Christ as preacher and healer had multiplied till "they fainted, and were scattered abroad, as sheep having no shepherd." Evidently the numbers had outgrown the physical capability of one to reach them all. Jesus directed the attention of his disciples to the situation and said to them, "The harvest truly is plenteous, but the laborers are few; pray ye, therefore, the Lord of the harvest that he will send forth laborers into his harvest." There is no reason to doubt that at least the more earnest of Christ's followers obeyed this injunction. They took the situation into their minds till, like their Master, they were filled with compassion for the needs of the multitude; then they earnestly prayed to God to furnish laborers for his own work. Perhaps during some at least of the hours of the night, while Jesus was praying on this subject on the mountain-top, St. John was awake praying about it at the foot of the mountain.

In the morning the answer came; but in what form?

THE DISCIPLE WHOM JESUS LOVED.

St. John was told to answer his own prayer; for he was called to be one of the laborers whom he had asked God to send. It was as if, in a period of destitution, a rich man, overcome with compassion for his poor and suffering fellow-creatures, should pray to God to succor them, and it should thereupon be flashed into his mind that he could himself relieve them by giving away a portion of his wealth. Thus are prayer and effort joined. If people have compassion on the multitude because they are scattered abroad, in our slums at home or in heathen lands, like sheep without a shepherd, and if they are earnestly praying the Lord of the harvest to send forth laborers, there will be no lack of either men or means for the Lord's service.

XV.

The dignity of this new position to which St. John was raised is clearly defined by St. Mark: "He ordained twelve, that they should be with him, and that he might send them forth to preach, and to have power to heal sicknesses and to cast out devils."

Here are three things which the apostles were to do: first, to be with him; secondly, to preach; and thirdly, to heal sicknesses and cast out devils.

The first, "that they should be with him," is the privilege for which all generations since have envied the Twelve. They went about with him continually; they saw all his miracles; they heard all his discourses; they daily listened to his table-talk, and could consult him about anything in his public utterances which they had not understood, or about which they wished to make further inquiry; they saw his life at close quarters, and felt the influence of his character. The followers of a Socrates, the catechumens of an Ambrose, the students of a Tholuck, the pupils of an Arnold, have informed the world of the magnetism with which their teachers held them; but no man ever spake and no teacher ever charmed like this One.

This privilege was not, indeed, new to St. John when he became an apostle; he had enjoyed it on the lower stage of discipleship. But it is emphasized at this stage to remind us that, in advancing to be an apostle, he did not leave behind the experiences peculiar to the two previous stages. He was first believer, then disciple, then apostle; but when he became an apostle he required to be far more than ever both believer and disciple. To be a public representative of Christianity is a mockery and hypocrisy unless it is accompanied with growing faith in Jesus and fellowship with him. Those who teach must not only have learned, but they must go on learning. The power of public testimony depends on intimacy with Jesus in secret.

Then, secondly, St. John and his fellow-apostles were to preach. This was rendered necessary by the extent of the interest in Jesus: his voice could not reach all who thronged around him, nor could he visit all the places which desired his presence; he had, therefore, to multiply himself by sending forth those who could speak in his stead; and the name he gave them showed that this was the chief object for which they were ordained; for the word "apostles" means "ambassadors." In one respect it might have been thought that they were unfit for this part of their vocation, because they were "unlearned and ignorant men;" they had not attended the colleges where the arts of the speaker are taught. For the present, however, their teaching was to be very simple. They were not to be settled for a length of time anywhere, but to itinerate swiftly from place to place. What they required, therefore, was not a system of doctrine, but a brief, fervent message; and this they had acquired from their contact with Jesus: their souls were on fire with a joyful discovery, and it was a pleasure to make it known.

At a later stage much more difficult work lay before the apostles, requiring resources of many kinds; but Jesus could trust to the educative power of their intercourse with himself. Nor was his confidence misplaced; for, when the time came, they were fit to be the teachers of the world.

Whether or not Jesus would have chosen learned men, if they had been available, we cannot say; the case of St. Paul, who had sat at the feet of Gamaliel, seems to suggest that he would. But such men were not forthcoming: men like Nicodemus and Joseph of Arimathea hesitated; and the scribes opposed and despised him. So he had to make use of such instruments as were procurable. But he was satisfied with them. These honest and good hearts, these unwarped and unbiassed minds, transmitted the message without coloring it with additions of their own; and it is easier for the world in their case to see that the excellency of the power was not theirs but his.

The third design of the apostolate was that its members should heal sicknesses and cast out devils. In some respects this was the most peculiar work of the apostles, though it was subordinate to their preaching; and it revealed in the most remarkable way the glory of their Master. In the gospels, Christ's powers of healing are attributed to the Spirit of God dwelling in him; but the Spirit dwelt in him so abundantly that the influence overflowed upon those who were in sympathetic contact with him; and, thus qualified, they were able, too, to cure both the body and the mind.

A great modern teacher, the devoted but romantic Edward Irving, cherished and propagated the notion that these powers would still be at the disposal of the Church if her members lived close enough to Christ. It was a mistake, though perhaps better than the orthodoxy of little minds. Experience has not justified his belief; and the reason, no doubt, is that such miraculous powers are no longer necessary. The spirit, however, of this direction of Jesus to his apostles is applicable to all times, and it is that the healing of the body is to accompany the saving of the soul. Not only may benefits conferred in the name of Christ in the sphere of the natural life open the door for spiritual work, but the interest in humanity taught by Christ extends to man's whole being and cannot help seeking to bless him at every point. When we send out medical along with preaching missionaries, when nurses are trained to be servants of the Church, when hospitals are opened by Christian liberality, when alms are given to the poor, when in connection with churches and missions wholesome recreation is provided for mind and body, we are following this indication of the mind of Christ; and in our day the Church is awaking to a more large-hearted conception of her duty in this respect.

In choosing the Twelve Jesus was determining not only their life but also his own. If they were to be with him, he was to be with them. He was not to have his time to himself, or even for the public; at least a large share of it was covenanted to the apostles. Nothing in his entire history is more wonderful than the way in which, while overwhelmed with external work, he reserved himself for the instruction of the Twelve. The results have abundantly justified his wisdom; and they supply an example, though one which has been rarely followed. Few even of the most earnest workers for the many have at the same time been able to think of the few. It requires rare gifts; yet a few followers highly trained, and acquainted with the deep things of God, may be a far more valuable legacy to the Church and the world than multitudes converted to a superficial or ordinary Christianity.

XVI.

The supreme privilege of the apostleship was to be with Jesus; but this involved another: it was also a privilege for each apostle to be associated with the other members of the apostolic circle.

Anyone who has been at college and entered thoroughly into the spirit of it must always look back to his student days as a golden period of his life; and the chief reason is that there he has associated with picked men. By a process of natural selection a large proportion of the most gifted and aspiring youth of the country gather in college; it is easy among them to find friends; and never again, perhaps, in life may a man be close to so many choice spirits. Much more true is it that the college of the apostles consisted of picked men. They had been selected by the insight of Christ himself, after a night of prayer and, no doubt, days of reflection. They were chosen from among his numerous followers as the most devoted to his person and the most suitable for his work. Their hearts were aglow with the joy of spiritual discovery and the enthusiasm of a noble cause. Could there be more favorable conditions for the formation and the ripening of friendship?

United, however, as the members of the apostolic circle were in their fundamental experiences and aspirations, they were nevertheless widely diverse in other respects. It would be difficult to conceive two characters by nature more unlike than St. Peter and St. John; St. Matthew, before his call, had been a publican—that is, a tax-gatherer for the Roman rulers—while one of the Simons had been a Zealot—that is, a radical opponent of the government, and especially the taxation, of the Romans; in the company of Jesus St. James the martyr and St. Thomas the doubter met together; and the less-known apostles in all probability represented similar diversities. It seems to have been the design of Jesus to unite in his service the most diverse talents and dispositions, and in this there was a special blessing for each of the Twelve; because those acquaintanceships and friendships are the best which, along with unity in essentials, combine the utmost variety in details.

One great intention of Christianity is to be a centre of union. Multitudes would be utterly lonely in the world were it not for their connection with the church; and many more, though enjoying other opportunities of union with their fellow-creatures, have found in the church their best friends and formed their most cherished ties. Christian work especially affords such opportunities: and nowhere else are the acquaintanceships formed likely to be so valuable, for attraction to the work of Christ is a selective process which winnows out the best.

XVII.

On this occasion St. John received from the Lord a special mark of recognition: he and his brother were called by a new name—Boanerges, the sons of thunder.

This is mentioned only by St. Mark and only in this place, and unfortunately the name is to us an enigma.

Some have explained it as an allusion to the origin of their spiritual life. They were disciples of the Baptist before becoming disciples of Christ; the Baptist's teaching was the seed from which their new destiny developed. Now his preaching might, for obvious reasons, be compared to thunder: it consisted chiefly of denunciations of sin and calls to repentance. It has further been suggested that St. John and St. James may have been in the company of the Baptist on the occasion when he received the sign by which he was assured that Jesus was the Christ; and one element of this was a voice from heaven, uttered, no doubt, in thunder. As this could not but affect the minds of the brothers they might be said to be born of the thunder.

The more common notion, however, has been that the name referred to some personal peculiarity. In common parlance the name Boanerges is applied to a speaker with a very loud voice; and this has actually been supposed to have been the reason why the name was given originally. A conspicuously loud voice is, however, about the last attribute which should be associated with St. John, and we cannot suppose Jesus to have laid any emphasis on such a trifling circumstance.

There has been much stronger support given to the notion that a mental peculiarity of the brothers was touched upon. There are several instances in their subsequent history—notably the occasion when they wished to call down fire from heaven on a town which refused to receive their Master—which indicate that in the earlier stages of development they were specially characterized by a fiery and excessive zeal. It is, indeed, difficult to reconcile with this image of St. John the charity and lovableness of his later years; but the fact seems to be undeniable. The Book of Revelation is the transfigured form of this disposition; and it is a book full of thunders, lightnings and voices from heaven. The character which is gentlest and most tolerant in maturity may have, hidden at its core, a temper once hot but long subdued by grace. The idea, then, is that Jesus was alluding to this imperfection of the two brothers, marking it with a name, that they might watch against temptation and overcome their failing. They did overcome it, and this accounts for the fact that the name occurs nowhere else; the peculiarity at which it pointed having disappeared it ceased to be applicable, and was forgotten.

The objection to this view is that, were it true, the name must have been a reproof, almost a nickname, but the names bestowed at similar crises throughout the Bible were all intended as marks of honor. So it was when Abram was changed to Abraham, Jacob to Israel, Simon to Peter, and so on. It is not agreeable to own that we are baffled, but the circle of conjecture in this case yields nothing decisive; and the best we can say is that the name probably conveyed to St. John and St. James some secret of the divine favor or some hint for their subsequent progress which we are not now in a position to define.

ST. JOHN ONE OF THREE.

XVIII.

St. John was, first of all, merely a believer in Christ. Then he was drawn into the narrower circle of Christ's disciples — that is, of those who gave up their occupations, and left all, to follow him whithersoever he went. Finally, he was elected one of the Twelve who were to be with Christ in a still closer way and to act as his heralds and ambassadors. But at this point his progress did not stop: even within the circle of the Twelve there was formed, by divine selection, a still narrower circle: three of the Twelve became, in a special sense, Christ's confidential friends, and St. John was one of the Three.

Are there not such distinctions still? The Christian name is a very wide word, and includes vast multitudes within its circumference. But Christians are not all alike: they are not all equally near to the Saviour; they are not all equally identified with his cause and his work. Some hearts in which the Gospel strikes root bear only thirty-fold, while others bear sixty-fold, and some bear a hundred; there is what may be called minimum Christianity, and there is average Christianity, and there is a Christianity which may be called maximum. A man may begin at the outer circle by being a minimum Christian; but he may pass inwards through one circle after another, still following the attraction of

Christ, till he gets as near to him and as like him as it is possible in this world to be. We ought not to be content with merely being able to claim the Christian name: if Christ is our Lord and Master, and if we have chosen him as our ideal and pattern, the true path of life must consist in being more and more absolutely identified with him.

The image of this close friendship, as we see it in the experience of the Three, of whom St. John was one, will answer such inquiries as these: Into what situations does such a friendship take men? Where are its trysting-places? By what experiences are men proved to be specially His friends?

The first scene in which we find the Three associated with Jesus is at the raising of the daughter of Jairus. The other apostles were in the street with their Master, but, when he arrived at the house, he permitted none to enter but Peter, James and John.

Thus the house of mourning was the first rendezvous. And none will ever be very near to Jesus who do not go to meet him there. Many who bear the Christian name never go. Although in so many of his sayings Jesus has made the visiting of the sick and dying, of the widow and the orphan, of the poor and needy, a conspicuous mark of his religion, yet the number of professing Christians is small who go upon such errands. Multitudes who would be indignant if their Christianity were called in question never, from January to December, enter the house of a poor person. They are not even aware where such persons are to be found; they would not know how to approach them;

they would be shocked at the sight of suffering and death; the world of misery is to them a *terra incognita*. To some Christians, however, it is well known. They are always in it. One case leads on to another. If only you are known as a friend and visitor of the poor appeals will come fast enough. It may appear an undesirable world to know—this world of misery; yet those who go about in it find many features to fascinate. Undoubtedly the most attractive, however, is that Christ is there. Nowhere else are you more certain of finding him or of being found by him.

The sight of so stupendous a miracle as the raising of a human being from the dead was a rare privilege, which the Three enjoyed by being with Jesus in the house of mourning. But perhaps it was for something else that he took them there; his own behavior on this occasion was a wonderful illustration of gentleness and delicacy of feeling and action.

When he arrived at the house death had already taken place, and the usual Jewish paraphernalia of mourning were in possession. The Oriental gives violent expression to his emotions; in grief he rends his garments, casts dust upon his head and clothes himself in sackcloth. And when the extreme sorrow of bereavement comes he even calls in outsiders to express his woe: professional mourners make doleful music and hired women utter piercing wails. This was all going on when Jesus arrived. But to him it was odious, as was everything unreal. He knew that this professional woe meant nothing; those who were weeping could as easily laugh; indeed, they did laugh the next minute, when he said that the maid was not dead. So, assuming the form of authority which he could wear so irresistibly when occasion required, he put them all forth, and thus produced the silence which, to his feeling, was the proper accompaniment of death.

Then, when peace reigned, he approached the room where death had pitched his tent. He bade the father and mother enter; it was their right. Then he admitted the Three: twelve would have disturbed his sense of congruity. Then he took her cold hand, that, when she awoke, she might be steadied, instead of being terrified, and might look up in his face and be comforted. After the miracle was over he ordered the parents to give her something to eat, that the expressions of wonder might not continue too long; and, under cover of their occupation with this duty, he, along with the Three, retired.

By his reverence for death, for maidenhood, for fatherhood and motherhood, and by his dislike of noise, unreality and rumor, Jesus was teaching the Three a part of his secret. It is not enough to do good deeds: to be like Christ, these must be done in the right manner — with delicacy, refinement and reticence. There are those who wish to do good, but they are so boisterous with it, or they talk so much about it, that what they do is robbed of all grace. There are those who display a keen interest in the eternal welfare of their neighbors, but they approach them with so little respect that they offend instead of winning. Such have only learned the one half of the secret of Jesus.

XIX.

The next scene in which the Three figure is the Transfiguration. In the evening Jesus took Peter, James and John up to a mountain apart, while the rest of the apostles were left below on the plain.

For what purpose were they thus taken into solitude? Knowing their Master's habits they could have no doubt, as they drew near the top and the shades of night were falling: they were going to pray; and he at least was still praying at the moment when the scenes of the Transfiguration commenced.

Those who live close to Jesus and are like him must often be with him in the school of prayer. All Christians pray; yet there are great differences. The prayers of many are brief and formal; they are a duty rather than a privilege; they are recollections from the past rather than the spontaneous outflowings of present emotion. But to some Christians prayer is vital breath; they talk with God as children with a father; they forget the flight of time, because they are absorbed and delighted. It was to spend a whole night on the height that Jesus invited the Three.

In hours of this kind wonderful things occur. To Jesus himself the Transfiguration may be said to have been a reward for the night of prayer. From the state of exaltation to which prayer had already raised him he passed, without a break, into the condition of transfiguration. He had reached a crisis of his life. For a long time at its commencement his ministry in Galilee had been extraordinarily successful—his miracles excited unbounded enthusiasm; his preaching drew countless multitudes; it seemed as if the unanimous voice of the nation were to carry him to the throne of his fathers. But of late a change had taken place—the popular feeling had cooled; opposition had risen in different quarters; Jesus had been compelled to withdraw himself from the impure zeal of the mob. He saw clearly in front the narrow way at the end of which stood the cross. More and more he had been retiring into himself. He was in need of support and encouragement. Often had he sought these in communion with the great spirits of the past, by whom his destiny of suffering had been foreseen and foretold. At length communion with them became so close that Moses and Elias, the representatives of law and prophecy, were drawn across the confines of the world invisible, and they conversed with him, no doubt to his great strengthening and comfort; about the decease which he was to accomplish at Jerusalem — the one event in Christ's earthly history on which is concentrated the interest of all the redeemed of mankind, and of all heaven itself.

Then ensued greater honor and comfort still, when the bright cloud, the symbol of the divine presence, enveloped the mountain-top, and out of it issued the voice of God himself, saying, "This is my beloved Son, in whom I am well pleased; hear ye him." It was a testimony which must have made his heart glad, that his mode of doing the work of his Father had, up to this point, been perfect and acceptable, and a pledge that the same grace would continue to sustain him during the portion of his obedience yet to come.

To the Three it was a great privilege to see their Master in this hour of exaltation. Two of them refer to it in their writings as a crowning mercy of their experience. St. Peter says, "He received from God the Father honor and glory . . . . when we were with him in the holy mount." And St. John is probably referring to the same incident when he says: "We beheld his glory, the glory as of the only-begotten of the Father." It was a preparation for them, too, in view of the trials to which their faith was to be exposed in the months when their Master was to be despised and rejected of men. When their Messianic hopes were disappointed, and the career of Jesus took a course totally different from that which they had anticipated, there was put on their faith a tremendous strain; but by what they had seen and heard on the Mount they were enabled to stand it, and to form the nucleus of loyalty round which the rest of the apostles gathered.

All who meet with Christ on the heights will, in some degree, share the same privileges. They will possess evidence of the glory of Christ not to be obtained elsewhere. Faith is in some minds a tradition handed down from the past which they have never doubted; in others it is a conviction laboriously hammered out by argument. But there is a faith which is more quick and powerful than these: it is the faith of experience; and it can hardly be missed by those who are much on the Mount. In such circumstances they receive evidence of God's existence, his glory and his love, which becomes part and parcel of their own being; and in such intercourse with the Saviour there cannot but occur now and then experiences of exaltation and revelation which are registered among the most precious memories of the past, and can only be taken away by some catastrophe which blots out the records of experience altogether.

XX.

The next occasion on which the Three were alone with Jesus was in Gethsemane. If it is natural to wish to have dear friends near in an hour of triumph, it is still more an instinct of the heart to wish this in the season of sorrow. Jesus invited the Three to the mountain-top that they might behold his glory; he invited them into the depths of the garden that they might support him in his hour of agony.

The soul of the Saviour was exceeding sorrowful, even unto death. The hour to which he had long been looking forward had arrived; but it proved to be intolerably bitter.

Grief has a double instinct: it seeks solitude; and Jesus removed himself a stone's cast even from the Three into the depths of the grove; yet, at the same time, it seeks sympathy; it is a relief to it to pour itself out into willing ears; and, therefore, Jesus wished them to be near, that he might go to them when the state of his overcharged heart would allow him. The disciples had need, besides, to pray on their own account. They, too, had reached a crisis in their fortunes, where they might suffer shipwreck, and again and again he urged them to watch and pray, lest they should enter into temptation.

It was a golden opportunity for the Three, when they could have obtained insight into the heart of their Master, and might have rendered him service which would have been divinely recompensed, besides preparing themselves for playing the man in the scenes which were about to ensue. But it was a lost opportunity. They were near him in Gethsemane; yet they were not with him. Jesus had invited them to a degree of confidence and intimacy beyond what they had ever yet enjoyed; but they could not enter so far into his secret. We wonder especially at St. John. He at least might have kept awake, although the other two had slept. He should have filled the place of the angel, who had to come from heaven to strengthen the Saviour because there was not a man to do it. St. John's loving and sensitive heart you would have expected to be all alive and awake, when he saw the state into which his beloved Master had fallen. But even he succumbed to the drowsiness of grief; and Jesus came, seeking sympathy and comfort, and found none. "Sleep on now," he said, "and take your rest." The opportunity was passed; and nothing could ever recall it.

Christ still invites us into Gethsemane. When may he be said to do so? When his cause appears to be in desperation; when the world is all against him, and his truth requires to be maintained against the organs of public opinion and the dead weight of conventionalism; when to confess him associates us with the poor and despised, while those whose good opinion we have been accustomed to enjoy wonder at us. In circumstances of this description a rare opportunity is offered of getting near to Christ. Never do we understand him so well, never does his love shine so full upon us, as when we are sacrificing honor, comfort, pleasure for his sake. But too often the opportunity is lost. Self-indulgence in some form comes in. It may not be a gross form: the sleep of the disciples in Gethsemane was very pardonable, and our self-indulgence may be something equally innocent. It may be the reading of a book when we ought to be saving a soul; it may be sitting in the comfort of home when we ought to be on the track of the homeless; it may be acquiescence in the opinions and practices of the respectable set to which we belong when we ought to come out from them and, at the risk of being thought odd, or even mad, offer our protest. A thing in itself entirely innocent may act as a soporific—to dull the sense of duty, and smother the call of Christ—so that the opportunity of being brought close to him through the fellowship of his sufferings is lost for ever.

XXI.

There is one more scene in which the Three appear along with Jesus, though on this occasion there was associated with them a fourth — St. Andrew, the brother of St. Peter; the same who in the lists of the apostles is always associated with the Three in forming the first group of four. On a day in the last week of our Lord's earthly life we find these four seated with Him on the Mount of Olives over against the Temple — that is, they were looking across the holy city, which lay at their feet, and they were thinking of the doom by which, Jesus had told them, it was to be overtaken — when they asked him, "Tell us, when shall these things be? and what shall be the sign when all these things shall be fulfilled?"

In thus asking they were exercising a privilege often used by the Twelve, to seek for an explanation of anything in their Master's doctrine which they had not understood, or the solution of any problem suggested to their minds by remarks which he had made. Probably this privilege had been specially exercised on other occasions by the Three. It was a very precious privilege, and on this occasion Jesus gave a very full and impressive answer.

It is a sign of advancement in the divine life to feel an interest in the mysteries of religion; and in this region Jesus meets those who have his mind. In our day, indeed, the desire is often expressed for a Christianity free from mysteries: would not the Sermon on the Mount, along with a simple outline of the facts contained in the gospels, be enough? can we not get quit altogether of dogmas and doctrines? Well, it is a very fair question how much ought to be demanded as a foundation for Christian union and coöperation. The quantum ought perhaps to be reduced to a minimum. If any man acknowledges Christ as his Lord and Saviour we need not ask much more about his creed before welcoming him as a Christian brother. But, while a minimum of belief may be enough to entitle a man to be called a Christian, a man cannot be an advanced or matured Christian without the necessity asserting itself within him for a more comprehensive creed. The Christian life, as it progresses, raises questions the answers to which are the doctrines of the gospel; and the deeper the life is the deeper will be the doctrines required to express it.

It is true that there is an intellectualism which separates dogma from life and substitutes the reasonings of the head for the experiences of the heart. There is also a prying into religious mysteries which is born only of morbid curiosity. There is, for example, a habit of speculating about the future which sometimes approaches the brink of insanity. But the caricature of a thing is no condemnation of the thing itself. On this occasion Christ did not tell the inquiring spirits by whom he was surrounded that such questions as they had put were of no moment. He gave a solemn and satisfying answer.

There are doctrines which are simply the intellectual equivalents for spiritual experiences, and where the experiences exist the truths which explain them will be understood and relished — while, on the other hand, contempt or impatience of these doctrines is an indication of the absence of the experiences. So a living interest in the progress of the kingdom of God gives an interest in the mystery of the future. You cannot break up a human nature into compartments and say that religion is to reside in some of them and not in others. Where religion is real and progressive it quickens the whole man. And not least does it affect the intelligence. The intellect is a noble faculty, and when, under the excitement of experience, it seeks to penetrate the mystery of life, He who is our wisdom, no less than our righteousness and sanctification, delights to answer its interrogations.

ST. JOHN'S BESETTING SIN.

XXII.

The destiny of St. John was to be near to Christ. From the outside world he entered first within the circle of Christ's disciples. From there he moved inwards, within the circle of the Twelve. Still he pressed nearer, being admitted into the circle of the Three. And, finally, he was the One whom Jesus loved.

It was a glorious destiny. Many a man would say that the greatest distinction of his life has been the set of friends he has known. Even a single friendship, with a specially gifted man or woman, may be the most golden memory of a life. But no friendship the world has ever seen can be compared with that enjoyed by St. John. To lie on the breast of the Son of man, to share his inmost thoughts, to be formed by daily and hourly contact with his personality—this was an unparalleled privilege.

Like all great privileges, however, it had its penalties. And one of these was the exposure of the disciple's weaknesses. None could come near to Christ without being dwarfed by his stature and darkened in his light. We see, especially in the final scenes of his life, how this happened to his enemies. One after another approached him—Judas, Caiaphas, Herod, Pilate and the rest—only to have every spot and wrinkle of his own character made everlastingly visible. But the same happened, in a different way, to his friends. No doubt Jesus drew forth all that was good in them; whatever seeds of promise their natures contained were rapidly developed by the influence of his companionship. But the evil in them was brought to light too. Sometimes, when a block of freestone is brought from the quarry and dressed in the sculptor's yard, it looks beautiful, but after it has been fitted into its place in the building the action of the weather has a strange effect. The stone begins to bleed, as the phrase is; its surface becomes covered with discoloring exudations. These proceed from iron or sulphur hidden in its interior; and the disfiguration may be so great that the stone has to be removed from its place altogether. The fellowship and work of Christ have a similar effect on his followers, bringing to the surface their concealed vices and unconscious weaknesses.

Weaknesses like those of St. John are especially tested by Christ's work. In human nature there are two opposite poles of sin, within which all the other forms of evil find their places. Where the constitution is soft and loose, the temptation is self-indulgence in its various forms; but where, on the contrary, the elements are finer and more compact, the danger lies in self-conceit, with all its developments of arrogance, ambition and intolerance. St. John's was a refined and reserved nature, and pride was his besetting sin. On this the work of Christ has an exciting effect, because it separates a man from his fellows and places him in a superior position. He possesses a secret which others do not share; he criticises their conduct from the height of his own ideal; he approaches them as a reprover and a revealer. Unless he has learned from some other quarter the secret of humility, his position may make him scornful and overbearing.

There is a legend of St. John's later life which, if it were true, would prove that this failing clung to him to the last. Meeting the heretic Cerinthus in the bath, it is said, he fled from the building, alleging as his reason that it was not safe to be under the same roof with such an enemy of God, because the judgment of God might at any moment destroy the building which contained him. But we will hope that the education imparted in the school of Christ had long before the arrival of old age made St. John more charitable in his judgments and more watchful of his words.

XXIII.

The most conspicuous occasion on which the tendency to pride showed itself in St. John's conduct was when, with his brother and his mother, he came to Jesus to petition him for a certain thing.

It is not clear whether the ambitious notion originated in the minds of the sons or in that of the mother. In one of the gospels the mother appears to take the initiative, bringing her sons to Jesus and prostrating herself before him, to ask on their behalf that they should sit, the one on his right hand and the other on his left, in his kingdom; but it is possible that she was only the catspaw through whom they sought their ambitious ends. If so, their design was well planned. A woman is a more effective petitioner than a man. Even the excess of pride in her sons which she may display has an amiable appearance and moves sympathy rather than antipathy. She no doubt approached Christ with a smile, and what in them might have looked offensive seemed admirable in her. Besides, she had claims. She was the aunt of Jesus, in all probability. She had been one of those women who in Galilee had followed him, ministering to him of their substance. Above all, she had given him her two sons, who had been among the very best of his followers. Salome was herself a true lover and disciple of Jesus. But her devotion to the cause was mixed with selfish elements; and, because her ambition was on behalf of

ST. JOHN'S BESETTING SIN.

her sons rather than herself, she may have indulged it with the less fear. She had not yet learned to know her Teacher well enough, or to feel how small all such selfish desires were to be made by the tragedy of his fate.

There can be no doubt, however, that her sons, though they kept in the back-ground, were quite as full of ambition. Indeed, in one of the gospels they are represented as presenting the petition on their own behalf; and this lets out the secret: the design was more theirs than hers. Some have discerned good elements in their ambition. It sprang, they think, from their desire to be near Christ; it showed at least their faith in his royal dignity and claims. "The juice of the ripe apple is the same," it has been remarked, "that it was in the green fruit, *plus* sunlight and sunheat." And it is true that what in youth is self-conceit and intolerance may, through maturing of experience and the influence of sanctification, grow into the dignity and stability of a self-respecting character. The self-suppression of St. John's later writings may be only the self-assertion of his youth in a ripened and sanctified form; and the intolerance of his youth may in his old age have mellowed into the firmness of principle and the perseverance of tireless love. But certainly at this early stage his ambition was of the earth, earthy; and its manifestation was both unlovely and hurtful.

One of its evil results was to inflame the rest of the apostles. When they heard the petition of James and John they were indignant. It seemed to them that the brothers were trying to take a mean advantage of them. And this was too true. Yet their own anger sprang from the same root. They also were dreaming of thrones and dignities. From other incidents we learn that the whole apostolic circle was at this time inwardly convulsed by such desires and disputes. Yet day by day Jesus was, at this very time, telling them that he was to suffer and die. Self was reigning in them, and so their eyes were blinded. He might have said to them, "My thoughts are not your thoughts, neither are your ways my ways."

XXIV.

He did speak to them on this occasion, and in words of great dignity and profundity set before them the contrast between the selfish spirit which they had been displaying and the true spirit of his kingdom; but he spoke with kindness and consideration, not in anger but in sorrow, for he knew how difficult was their situation and how little they were yet able to take in the truth: nothing but events could disabuse their minds of the prejudices in which they were held.

"Ye know not what ye ask," he said to the brothers. Their petition was that they might be on his right hand and on his left; but his prophetic eye, looking forward to the crisis which now arrested his attention whenever he thought of the future, saw on his right hand and on his left—what? On each hand a cross, with a victim upon it. To be in the place of the two thieves, crucified with him, was what they were asking, if they had only known.

The favorites of a king, seated on his right hand and on his left, may have the privilege of drinking out of the royal cup and dipping their fingers or napkins in the vessel in which he washes his hands; and James and John had had this honor in their thoughts. But the thoughts of Jesus flew forward to a cup of which he was to drink, and a laver in which he was to bathe; but the cup was his agony, and the laver the bath of his own blood. With deep emotion he, therefore, asked, "Are ye able to drink my cup and be baptized with my baptism?" "Yes," they replied, "we are able," not knowing what they said. And again, as his prophetic eye glanced into the future, he added, "Ye shall, indeed, drink of my cup and be baptized with my baptism;" for he foresaw that St. James was to fall a martyr under the sword of Herod, and he knew by what manner of death St. John was to glorify God.

"But," he added, "to sit on my right hand and on my left is not mine to give, but it shall be given unto them for whom it is prepared of my Father." These words sound like a limitation of the knowledge and authority of Jesus; as if this were one of those mysterious things which, he declared on another occasion, the Father had kept in his own hand. But probably the meaning is simple. Salome and her sons had asked Jesus to bestow the honors of his kingdom in answer to their petition. Such was the bad practice of Oriental monarchs: they gave places away to favorites capriciously, without regard to services or merits. Jesus says there is to be in his kingdom no such favoritism or giving away of positions: every post will be given to the man for whom it has been prepared, or to the man who has been prepared for it. The man on whom God has conferred the necessary gifts and graces, and who, employing well his talents in a few things, has qualified himself for being entrusted with many things—to him will the place of honor be given.

In addressing the Twelve Jesus made this contrast still more clear and emphatic. The way of earthly monarchies is that birth gives position, and he who has the position uses it for his own pleasure and aggrandizement; his station is measured by the numbers who are ready to bow to him and serve him. In the kingdom of God the ruling principle is exactly the reverse. Greatness is measured not by the number of those who serve you, but by the number of those whom you serve, and by the value of the services you render them. A high position is to be coveted, not because it confers ease or fame, but because it supplies the opportunity of doing more extensive good.

Never, surely, did Christ utter a more revolutionary word or characterize more clearly the difference between the world and Christianity. For what are the men and women of the world toiling, moiling and striving? To see who shall be uppermost; who shall command and control others; who shall be flattered and feared. But that, says Jesus, is not greatness: he is great who makes the world a wholesome and sunny place for others, and who, by the sacrifice of his own happiness, if necessary, makes others rejoice. Who is king of men and queen of women? He and she who make the greatest number good and glad.

How slowly the world learns this lesson! How slowly the Church learns it! Yet it is the lesson of the life of Christ. Why is he the greatest among the children of men? Because he took the whole human race into the embrace of his beneficence, and because the blessing which he conferred on them was the greatest of all—the gift of salvation. "The Son of man came to minister, and to give His life a ransom for many."

XXV.

There was another occasion on which St. John showed the same infirmity of temper. It came out during a scene of indescribable beauty in the life of Christ. Among the disciples there had been a dispute which of them should be the greatest; and their Master, knowing their thoughts, took a child and set him in the midst; then, clasping him in his arms, he proceeded to speak to them of the childlike spirit which they ought to cultivate, and of the danger of doing any offense to one of his little ones.

As the discourse proceeded in this strain, some of its words struck upon the conscience of one of the listeners. It was St. John, who remembered an incident of the recent past which seemed to be placed in a new light by what the Master was saying. Perhaps even at the time he had been doubtful about it; but now he was convinced that he had done wrong; so he made his confession. And it is to his honor that he was so prompt both to feel the prick of conscience and to make a public acknowledgment of his mistake.

The story was that, on a certain occasion when they were separate from their Master, the apostles had fallen in with one who was casting out devils in his name; and they had forbidden him, because he followed not with them: he did not belong to the company of Jesus. It is interesting to learn that faith in Christ had thus spread sporadically, outside the circle round about

ST. JOHN'S BESETTING SIN. 89

himself, and that it was strong enough even to cast out devils in his name. In a similar way we find the teaching of the Baptist taking root far from the scene of his labors and apart from the regular succession of his disciples.

But St. John and his companions had forbidden this humble and imperfect believer. It was a good work in which he was engaged, for surely the more victims could be delivered from the power of the devils the better, but they discovered some irregularity in his method of procedure; though he had the power of the Spirit he lacked the proper legitimation. Therefore, it seemed to them, he was poaching on their preserves, and with the pride of authority they silenced him.

It is pitiable to think, with this standing in the gospels, how often the same mistake has been repeated—how often the officials of the church have silenced testimony or stamped out good work inspired by the Spirit of God, because it has seemed to them to be in some way out of order or destitute of authority; how this or that branch of the church has considered itself the only legitimate one; and how the good of one section of the church has been evil spoken of by the rest.

On the other hand, it would be vain to deny that toleration is one of the most difficult virtues to exercise. It is not easy to find the golden mean between Sadducean laxity on the one hand and Pharisaic censoriousness on the other. We may be censuring the disciples at the safe distance of the centuries and doing the same thing ourselves.

Yet Jesus laid down on this occasion a broad rule:

"He that is not against us is for us." On another occasion he said precisely the reverse: "He that is not for us is against us." How shall we reconcile these opposite maxims? It is not difficult: obviously the one is a rule for judging others, the other a rule for judging ourselves. When we are criticising our own conduct we should be stern and searching and this word should sound in our souls: "He that is not with me is against me;" but when we are criticising the conduct of others we ought to be lenient and charitable, remembering this word: "He that is not against us is for us." We know the motives of our own actions and the feelings which follow them; but we do not know the motives and feelings of others.

> "One point must still be greatly dark:
>   The reason why they do it;
> And just as lamely can we mark
>   How far perhaps they rue it.
> Then at the balance let's be mute,
>   We never can adjust it;
> What's done we partly may compute,
>   We know not what's resisted."

XXVI.

The third case in which St. John's arrogance and heat of temper came out was during the last journey to Jerusalem.

Jesus was passing from town to town, as he journeyed towards the capital, healing the sick and proclaiming the kingdom of God; and it seems to have been his practice to send on messengers in advance, to place after place, to announce his coming and perhaps also to make some provision for the entertainment of himself and his company. Two of these messengers were sent to a Samaritan village; for his road lay through Samaria; but they were met by an outburst of fanatical ill-feeling: the Samaritans would not receive them because they were on their way to Jerusalem.

The Jews had no dealings with the Samaritans; the Samaritans worshipped "in this mountain," but the Jews considered that Jerusalem was the place where men ought to worship. The rivalry was ancient and bitter, and at any moment it was liable to break out. The hatred of the Samaritans not infrequently vented itself on the Jewish pilgrims going to the feasts at Jerusalem; and it was in this character that Jesus and the apostles appeared to the Samaritan villagers on this occasion.

But the apostles were furious: this was an insult to them and an insult to their Master; whose greatness these rude fanatics wholly ignored. James and John especially distinguished themselves by their zeal; and they asked their Master, "Shall we call down fire on them from heaven, as did the prophet Elijah?" It was a strange question. There was in it the pride of miraculous power: they were confident that they could have produced the lightning. Yet almost unconsciously they felt that their proposal was unchristlike; for they did not ask him to do it, but said, "Shall we call down fire?" Very significant was their appeal to Elijah. This prophet had once brought down fire from heaven in Samaria; and their thought was justified to their own minds by appealing to so great an example.

Yet it was the old man in them that was speaking. It was, indeed, the same provincial and fanatical spirit as had spoken in the refusal of the Samaritans to entertain them. The old race hatred between Jews and Samaritans had blazed up in their hearts, attempting to wield the weapons of Christ and to wear the mantle of Scripture. How often have such passions—between Guelph and Ghibelline, for example, or between Roman-catholic and Orangeman—made the same attempt, speaking the pious language of religion and quoting the sanction of Scripture. Men have mistaken their own evil passions for the inspiration of the Spirit of God, and have believed themselves to be doing God service when they have let loose the demons of persecution, harrying innocent countries with fire and sword, and driving to the gallows and the stake men and women often a thousand times better than themselves.

But Jesus at once put his foot on this strange fire, with which his apostles sought to honor him. "Ye know not," he said, "what manner of spirit ye are of." This may mean, "Ye know not what spirit has at present possession of you; you think it is the spirit of religion, but it is the spirit of evil, masquerading in its clothes." Or it may mean that they were yet imperfectly acquainted with the spirit which, as his followers, they ought to cultivate. They had appealed to Elijah, one of the foremost representatives of the old covenant; but they ought to be aware that they were now under a better covenant. The spirit of the old dispensation was legal and stern; the spirit of the new was love. "The Son of man came not to destroy men's lives, but to save them."

This is the supreme rule and example; although they had not yet seen the supreme effort of their Master's forgiving love. If ever anyone was entitled to feel resentment against his fellow-creatures, it was the Son of God; justly might he have cursed and blighted the human race. But instead of doing so he gave his life for the world. We may ourselves, like these surly Samaritans, have refused to entertain him, keeping him out of our heart and refusing to have him to reign over us. Yet he has not ceased to love us; he is still waiting to be gracious. And it is when we have recognized how magnanimous and forgiving he is to us that we learn the lesson of forgiveness. Having obtained so great mercy we learn to be merciful.

It is strange to think that St. John was ever a prey to such passions as ambition, intolerance, and persecuting zeal—he whose very name is now a synonym for love. But it is an encouraging fact: it shows what changes grace can work. Intercourse with Christ transfigured St. John. Above all, he was altered by the passion of his Lord: the sight of that self-sacrifice for the sake of enemies made all resentful feelings die out of him; in the cross he saw that love alone is great, and he could not hate his brother man any more. The cross of Christ is the school of charity.

THE DISCIPLE WHO LOVED JESUS.

XXVII.

St. John was the disciple whom Jesus loved, but he was also the disciple who loved Jesus. All the disciples, with the exception of Judas, loved the Lord, just as He loved them all; but, as he bore to St. John a peculiar love, so the love of this apostle for him was peculiarly deep and faithful.

Of this, indeed, there is in the earlier passages of St. John's history little evidence; some passages even appear to betray an unusually selfish temper. But his affection for his Master must have been organizing itself in the depths of his nature, and at length it broke somewhat suddenly into flower. Sometimes love is thus brought suddenly to a head. It may never have been confessed, it may not even have come to consciousness in the heart itself till some unexpected turn of circumstances supplies the opportunity, when all at once it overflows the heart in a passion of desire, and at the same time makes itself known by word or act.

Among such occasions misfortune is not an unusual one. To see the person beloved in a position of dire need calls forth chivalrous devotion; reticence is forgotten, and personal considerations are thrown to the winds; the lover stands forth, avowing his passion before the world and ready to bear or to do anything which the interests of the object of his affection may require. Such were the circumstances in which St. John's love for Jesus came to full maturity and manifestation; it was in the four-and-twenty hours before the death on the cross that he showed how much he loved the Saviour.

The first scene of the kind took place in the upper room during the evening of the Last Supper, before the Lord fell into the hands of his enemies.

The feet-washing had taken place, and, the dispute which had given occasion to it having been composed, the Twelve were at last arranged round the table to begin the evening meal. They reclined on couches, each resting on his left elbow with his feet outstretched towards the back of the couch, so that the back of the head of his next neighbor was at each one's breast. St. John had the place immediately in front of Jesus, on whose breast he therefore leaned. It was a place apparently conceded instinctively to him by the rest, perhaps expressly appointed by Christ himself. It afforded opportunity, at all events, for closer fellowship than was conceded to the others.

Jesus had produced peace among the Twelve; but he was not at peace within himself, and his conversation could not flow as it did later in the evening. As the dove shivers when the hawk appears in the sky, or the horse stops and is bathed in perspiration when a snake lies across its path, so the spirit of Jesus was troubled, because in this scene about to be dedicated to friendship and religious exaltation there was an element entirely

THE DISCIPLE WHO LOVED JESUS. 97

foreign and hostile. With the false heart of Judas in the room the spirits of Jesus could not rise; and at last he was forced to let out the secret: "Verily, verily, I say unto you that one of you shall betray me."

The word fell like a bombshell among the guests, and instantly every one looked into the eyes of his neighbor to see the signs of guilt. Judas must have had a mind thoroughly schooled in the art of dissimulation to be able to remain unmoved beneath these searching glances; but he did not betray himself with the faintest blush or the least quiver of a lip. It speaks well for the honest hearts of the rest that they had never suspected him; they were not forward to think evil of a brother. Even now each rather doubted himself; and they began to ask in turn, "Lord, is it I?"

At last, however, St. Peter, who happened to be placed down the table at a distance from Jesus, signified by a gesture to St. John to ask the Master who was to be the betrayer. This was a significant act. It was the acknowledgment by St. Peter of St. John's primacy in the love and confidence of Christ. It was a tribute from the man of action to the man of contemplation. Those who are most prominent in the outer work of the Church must sometimes be indebted to the less conspicuous disciples, who lie in the bosom of the truth and brood on its hidden mysteries.

St. John asked the question in a whisper. Jesus might have kept the secret, sparing Judas till the last moment, but he whispered back, "He it is to whom I shall give a sop, when I have dipped it;" and he gave it to Judas. Two now knew the terrible secret.

Jesus had relieved his heart of its burden by making John partaker of it.

Judas knew that John knew; and this may be why it is said that, after the sop, Satan entered into him. He had long been aware that Christ knew what was going on in his mind, but he could keep his countenance as long as his treachery was concealed from his fellow-disciples. Now, however, when Jesus had told John, he was unmasked; and he was frantic. He hated Jesus for telling; he hated John for knowing; and when, immediately afterwards, he received the opportunity from a word of Christ he rushed out to carry into execution his diabolical design.

"And it was night," says the historian, with tragic brevity. The son of darkness had entered his own element and was reeling blindly down to his doom, while within the chamber, now relieved of his presence, all darkness vanished away, and during the hours which ensued the disciples were sitting in the light eternal. Of St. John especially may this be said. Are not he and Judas the extreme opposites? The same incident which drove forth Judas to his fate installed John more firmly than ever in the confidence and affection of his Master.

XXVIII.

THE second scene in which the love of St. John was displayed was immediately after the arrest of the Lord.

At the gate of Gethsemane, when Jesus fell into the hands of the soldiers sent to take him, all the disciples forsook him and fled. This may be a general statement, admitting of exceptions; just as the fourth Gospel says, in reference to the words in which Christ gave Judas his dismissal, "No man at the table knew for what intent he spoke this unto him," although it is manifest that St. John knew. In the same way this disciple may be an exception to the statement that all forsook their Master and fled. At all events, if St. John fled, his desertion must have been of the briefest possible duration; because immediately afterwards he, with St. Peter accompanying him, is seen following the procession to the palace of the high-priest; and he was in time to pass into the house, in the rear of the procession, before the gate was shut.

He had an advantage over his fellow-disciples which served him in good stead upon this occasion—he was known to the high-priest. In what way this acquaintance had been formed we have no information; conjecture has, however, been busy to fill up the blank. Some have found here an indication that the apostle had higher family connections than his station in life would naturally suggest, while others have thought that he may have been known to the high-priest through his business. There was a market in Jerusalem for the harvest of the Sea of Galilee; and there is no difficulty in believing that the family of Zebedee, or the firm to which they belonged, may have had an agency for the sale of their property in the capital. We really know nothing whatever on the subject, beyond the fact stated in the Gospel. Apparently, however, John knew not only the high-priest but his servants, and he was acquainted with the palace; and his familiarity in the place served as a passport, admitting him to the close neighborhood of Christ, where he wished to be. Had he, indeed, been more timid about his own safety than anxious to be near his Master, the fact that he was known to the high-priest might have operated in precisely the opposite direction. He might have been afraid of being recognized as a follower of Jesus; and his very hesitation might have led to the consequences which he dreaded. Boldness in a critical situation is half the battle; and love made John bold.

In St. Peter we see the working of the opposite state of mind. Perhaps from the first his heart was rather with those who fled than with St. John; but John constrained him. Some hesitation at all events is indicated by the fact that he was shut out of the palace when St. John was shut in. But the more loving disciple was eager to keep Peter up to the mark; and so he returned to the gate and secured his admission. Thereby, however, he unwittingly did his friend an injury. He was forcing on him an effort of testimony for which he was not prepared; he was introducing him to a temptation which was too strong for his powers of resistance; and the result was disastrous.

Then was made manifest how far St. John was ahead of St. Peter. He probably attended the trial throughout, and his silent presence was a support and comfort to Jesus, while Peter was showing what extraordinary elements existed in him under the covering of his Christian discipleship—profanity, falsehood and selfish fear.

What made so great a difference? Of two friends of Alexander the Great the historian Plutarch calls one Philo-Basileus, that is, the friend of the king, and the other Philo-Alexandros, that is, the friend of Alexander. Similarly some one has said St. Peter was Philo-Christos, the friend of the Christ, but St. John was Philo-Jesus, the friend of Jesus. This touches the quick: Peter was attached to the person who filled the office of Messiah, John to the Person himself. And this is a distinction which marks different types of Christian piety in all ages. The Christ of some is more official—the Head of the Church, the Founder of Christianity, and the like — that of others is more personal; but it is the personal bond which holds the heart. The most profoundly Christian spirits have loved the Saviour, not for his benefits, but for himself alone.

XXIX.

It is probable that St. John attended Christ through all the weary stages of his double trial—before the ecclesiastical and the civil authorities—and that, after a night thus spent, he accompanied the procession in the forenoon to the place of execution and witnessed everything that followed. At all events in the afternoon "there stood by the cross of Jesus his mother and his mother's sister, Mary the wife of Cleophas, and Mary Magdalene;" and with these holy women, one of whom was in all probability his own mother, stood St. John.

Striking it is that, in this hour of peril, when the men of Christ's following were conspicuous only by their absence, the women were so loyal and fearless; and the only man who stood with them was the most womanly spirit in the apostolic company. But there is an infinite difference between the feminine and the effeminate. Woman may in some respects be weaker than man, but she is stronger in love; and it was in the strength of his love that John was like a woman, while in mind and character he was a thorough man. The women may have been protected by their sex; he had no such protection, and yet he was there. No doubt in the service of Christ all kinds of power are necessary, and the masculine virtues have a part of their own to play; but for the supreme efforts of sacrifice and devotion which Christianity requires it must always ultimately depend on the strength of love.

Amid the howling sea of evil passions with which his cross was encompassed the dying eyes of the Saviour rested with a sense of profound relief on this little group of loyal and loving-hearts. But it is specially told that his glances rested on his mother and his favorite disciple. These were the two dearest souls to him on earth, and his eyes lingered on them. It was not, however, with unmixed satisfaction that he looked on his mother. This was for her an hour of unspeakable pain. It was not only that she was losing a son, and such a son, but her faith in God was subjected to a terrible strain. The event of her life had been the birth of him who, the angel had told her, would sit on the throne of his father David; but here he was expiring, and this promise had not been fulfilled! Was it a lie? The universe was swimming round her, and the sword of which the aged Simeon had spoken was piercing her soul. Besides, humbler anxieties about her troubled her son. He had been her support; but where would she now find a home? Who would now cheer and comfort her? Her other sons were still unbelievers.

At last he spoke. Indicating St. John with his eye, because he could not do it with his finger, he said to Mary, "Woman, behold thy son;" and, indicating him in the same way to her, he said, "Behold thy mother."

Thus he gave them to one another, as mother and son, with the solemnity with which in marriage husband and wife are given to each other, or as a dying person may sometimes indicate to two, standing beside the bed, that they ought to become one. They were kindred spirits in many respects, and especially they were one in their love to him. To none could Mary speak so freely about her son as to this loving disciple; from no one else could John learn so much as from her about Him whom to know is, as he declares, life eternal.

To Mary this was a splendid gift. It assured to her a home for the rest of her days in which she would breathe the same peaceful and hallowed air as Jesus had breathed into the home at Nazareth, and it gave her the protection of a Greatheart to stand between her and the world. To St. John it was a gift no less precious. Mary, on her own account, would have been an adornment to any home; but, even if her presence had involved inconvenience, she would still have been thrice welcome to him as the mother of his divine Friend. Friend? Jesus had called his own mother "thy mother;" was not this to adopt him as a brother? This was a supreme honor: and all the trouble which it might involve was light to a heart which loved with such fervor as his.

XXX.

It is generally supposed that at once St. John gently removed Mary from the scene of suffering and took her to his house in the city, which was thenceforth to be her home; and there, it is said, he cherished her for twelve years, refusing to leave Jerusalem, even for the purpose of preaching the gospel, till she died. But after he had safely deposited his precious charge in his home he hurried back to Calvary. By this time all was over. The execution was finished and the crowd had dispersed. Only a few soldiers were left, watching the bodies. St. John again, however, resumed his station at the foot of the cross of his beloved Master.

His fidelity was rewarded with a sight which profoundly impressed him, and which he has recorded with unusual solemnity. After narrating the incident he adds, "And he that saw it bare record, and his record is true; and he knoweth that he saith true, that ye might believe."

In Deuteronomy there is a law to this effect: "If a man have committed a sin worthy of death, and he be put to death, and thou hang him on a tree, his body shall not remain all night upon the tree, but thou shalt in any wise bury him that day (for he that is hanged is accursed of God); that thy land be not defiled which the Lord thy God giveth thee for an inheritance." Perhaps this rule was not always observed, and the Jews might be careless about it when executions in their country were carried out not by themselves but by the Romans. But the death of Jesus happened at a season when they were particularly scrupulous about anything which might defile, especially in the neighborhood of the Holy City. It was the Passover, and they besought the governor to have the bodies taken down and buried before sunset. Before this could be done, however, it was necessary that they should be dead; and crucified persons did not die so quickly. The Jews asked, therefore, that the life of the three crucified men should be extinguished by breaking their legs with clubs; and the governor consented that this should be done. When, however, the soldiers came to Jesus they perceived that he was dead already; so that they did not break his legs. But, by way of making assurance doubly sure, one of the soldiers plunged his spear into his side, whereupon there flowed out blood and water.

Such was the sight which so impressed the apostolic onlooker. But what was it which made it appear to him remarkable?

He recalled a word of the Old Testament which said, "A bone of Him shall not be broken." Originally it referred to the paschal lamb; and to St. John the dead Saviour was thus pointed out as the true Paschal Lamb, whose sacrifice should inagurate a new dispensation of grace and truth, as the original paschal lamb inaugurated the dispensation of the Law. Also he recalled another Old Testament word, which said, "They shall look upon Him whom they have pierced;" and there seemed to him to be a divine purpose guiding even the hand of the rude soldier, when, totally without his own will and knowledge, he brought the mode of Christ's death into line with Old Testament prophecy.

But the mystery did not stop here. Probably St. John was aware that from a dead body, if it is pierced, there is, as a rule, no outflow; but in this case there flowed out blood and water. It was a mystery; but in it there seemed to be a symbol of much that Christ had taught about himself. The cleansing of the world from sin had been the purpose of his life; and he had spoken of the cleansing power of water and the cleansing power of blood. The two sacraments which he instituted referred respectively to these two elements. The dead body of Christ appeared to be a double fountain, out of which was issuing what was required for the purification of the world.

Modern medicine, however, believes that it sees in the phenomenon which St. John has reported a significance which even he did not perceive. Great medical authorities allege that the stream of blood and water shows that the heart of Christ had ruptured at his death and the blood poured into an enclosing sac, where it would naturally resolve into its elements— one red like blood and the other white like water—and that it was this sac which the spear emptied. So that the Saviour literally died of a broken heart. The pressure of grief, the pressure of the burden of sin which he was bearing, so overcharged his heart that it could no longer contain; and, when it broke, he died.

However this may be, St. John was amply rewarded for his vigil of love. Love kept him near Christ living and dying; and to be near Christ is to be in the place of discovery. We are reminded how much we owe to St. John for his faithful love as often as we sing,

> " Let the water and the blood
> From thy riven side which flowed
> Be of sin the double cure:
> Cleanse me from its guilt and power."

ST. JOHN AND THE RESURRECTION.

XXX.

It is difficult for us to realize the dismay with which the death and burial of Jesus affected his followers. When we see him breathing his last, and the stone rolled to the door of his sepulchre, we are not afraid; for we know what is going to happen—that on the third day he is to rise again. At the time, however, none knew this.

His enemies had, indeed, heard of his prophecies to this effect, but of course they did not believe them; and when they saw the spear thrust into his side they thought that all was over with him and his cause: he would never trouble them any more. His whole career appeared to them ridiculous. He had been a candidate for the grand office of the Messiah, whom the nation was expecting. There had, however, been other candidates before him, whose attempts had come to nothing; and his pretensions were perhaps the least considerable of all. The Messiah whom they looked for was to be a prophet, a priest and a king in one, but most of all a king; to liberate them from bondage and lift up the country into everlasting power and renown. Jesus of Nazareth had, in their eyes, utterly failed to fulfil this ideal. He was of lowly birth, and his followers were few and humble like himself; he made a reputation for a time in the provinces, but never had aroused the enthusiasm of Jerusalem; at last, coming into collision with the authorities of the nation, he had gone down without a single blow being struck on his behalf. His name was only one more added to the list of fictitious messiahs.

Not only, however, did his enemies judge thus; the faith even of his friends was completely shattered. It is true, he had told them repeatedly beforehand that he was to die and the third day rise again. But these statements had made no impression on their minds and were no comfort to them when the crisis arrived: if they noticed them at all, they thought that their Master was speaking in parables, and they understood his words in a figurative sense. To the very last they believed that he was to be a great king, reigning over the house of Jacob for ever; and when his death rendered this impossible their faith was killed outright.

If it survived at all, it was in the form of love. They still loved him. They might, indeed, have felt that they had been deceived, and this feeling might have made them turn with resentment upon the memory of their buried Master; but, with the exception of Judas, they had been too completely captivated, and their hearts could not quickly cool towards One whom they had so many reasons for loving.

In Mary Magdalene we see this triumph of love over the disenchantment of events. In tradition this woman is identified not only with the woman who was a sinner and anointed the feet of Jesus, but also with Mary the sister of Martha and Lazarus; so that the traditional image of her is exceedingly rich and affecting. In reality she is identical neither with the one of these nor the other; and what we know of her is but limited. Seven devils went out of her at the command of Jesus; so that she had ample ground for deathless gratitude to him. Apparently she was a lady of property; for she, along with other honorable women, ministered of her substance to Jesus. The position assigned her among these women perhaps suggests that the place which she held in his affection and confidence was distinguished; and this is still more forcibly suggested by the interview accorded to her alone by the risen Saviour. At all events we may infer the fervor of her love from the fact that, after the Sabbath was past, she set out for the tomb before the break of day.

But for what was she going to the sepulchre? Not to see if he had fulfilled his prophecy that he would rise again, but to help to anoint his corpse for its long sleep. When she arrived at the sepulchre she saw the stone rolled away; but what did this suggest to her? Not that he was risen; of this she had not the most distant surmise; but that a horrible outrage had been perpetrated on the feelings of all who loved him: as she expressed it, "They have taken away the Lord, and we know not where they have laid him."

That her state of mind was that of all the rest of the followers of Jesus—an absolute blank, as far as any thought or hope of his rising was concerned—is amply proved. When the holy women to whom the risen One had shown himself returned to their fellows, "their words seemed to them as idle tales, and they believed them not." The report of the two to whom he appeared on the way to Emmaus met with a similar reception; and what could more significantly indicate the general state of mind than the pathetic words of those two themselves before he was made known to them: "We trusted that it had been he who should have redeemed Israel." Thomas' determination not to believe is well known; and even of the five hundred to whom the Lord showed himself in Galilee "some doubted." In short, the universal belief among his followers, when he was lying in Joseph's tomb, was, that his career was over and his enterprise at an end.

XXXI.

THERE are few things which move human beings more than the suspicion that there has taken place any tampering with the remains of their dead. An entire community can be convulsed with indignation at the mere rumor that a grave has been disturbed. Mary Magdalene was under the impression that the tomb of her beloved Lord had been rifled; and it was in a tumult of grief and indignation that she ran to bring word to the disciples.

She directed her steps to Peter and John; and soon she had them in earnest consultation on the subject. Whether Peter's denial of his Lord was known to Mary Magdalene or not, we cannot tell; but there can be little doubt that it was known to John, who was in the palace of the high-priest at the time when it took place. But this knowledge did not prevent John from meeting his comrade on the old terms. Possibly Peter, after weeping bitterly by himself, had sobbed out his contrition on the bosom of the disciple whom Jesus loved; and John's forgiveness may have been to him a confirmation of the forgiveness of the Lord.

Mary Magdalene's communication awoke in the two apostles a tumult of emotion as great as her own: they thought that the enemies of their Master, not content with the shame and injustice wreaked on him during his trial and crucifixion, had, in anger that he should have been laid by loving hands in an honorable grave, perpetrated on his corpse some new indignity; and they immediately set out to the spot to ascertain what had taken place. As they went, so hot were their hearts within them that they began to run; and soon they were running at full speed. There are moments in life when decorum is thrown to the winds, and everything is cast aside which stands in the way of an overmastering purpose. It shows how wild was the grief of the apostles, that they thus flew to their object.

In this crisis, when nature had her way with them, the characteristic differences between the two men showed themselves. The "other disciple did outrun Peter and came first to the sepulchre." Why was this? It has been conjectured that it was because Peter was older: John had the lightness and fleetness of youth. Or it has been thought that Peter was delayed by his penitence, the memory of his denial clogging his feet like a weight of lead. This motive would only have acted, however, had he thought that he was on his way to a meeting with Jesus, and there is not the slightest reason for thinking that any such expectation had crossed his mind. It was because John was the disciple of love that he arrived first at the sepulchre; for love lends wings, and its tension gave John the advantage.

At the sepulchre, however, Peter's temperament gave him the advantage. John, though he arrived first, remained outside. The stone was rolled away, but awe arrested him at the threshold; and all he ventured to do was, with hand over eyes, to gaze into the obscurity; and from this standpoint he could not see all that required to be seen in order to learn the true state of the case. Like Mary Magdalene, he saw in the rocky opening the sign of a deed of darkness, instead of the passage through which hope was about to break. But Peter, when he arrived, at once went in and encouraged John to follow. This was like the practical spirit of the man, who was not impeded with the finer sensibilities of his comrade; and on this occasion, at least, such boldness was what was required.

In the spiritual life, as in the natural, ghosts are frequently laid by boldly advancing on them. Only enter what looks like the yawning mouth of calamity, and you may find yourself in the sunshine of glorious discovery. Many a one, for example, is trembling before the spectre of religious doubt who, if he would only go forward, determined to find out exactly how much is in the objections which he fears, would discover that they melt away when closely examined, and in the very place haunted by them he would find the strongest confirmation of faith. Is not death to many all their lifetime like a gloomy opening into the unknown, before which they fear and quake? Yet if they would boldly examine the reasons why they fear, and the reasons which a Christian has for despising death, or even glorying in it, they might be emancipated from their bondage and enabled to serve the Lord with gladness and singleness of heart.

Let us take John for our instructor in the swiftness of love, and Peter for our teacher in courage.

XXXII.

So the two apostles stood inside the sepulchre. An ancient tomb was a spacious place, in which it was possible to stand erect and to move about; and, when their eyes had become accustomed to the obscurity, or they had placed themselves in a position to obtain the help of the light streaming in through the open doorway, they saw what astonished them.

The body, indeed, was not there; but objects presented themselves to view which at once exploded the hypothesis to account for its absence which Mary Magdalene had suggested, and with which their minds had been preoccupied as they ran to the sepulchre. The grave-clothes were lying where the body had been. Why should these have been left behind if the body had been stolen? If in wanton rage his enemies had stripped them off there would have been evidence of violence in their torn and disarrayed condition. But the reverse was the state of the case. The clothes were lying in perfect order, as if they had been put off in a leisurely and orderly way by him who had worn them. And their attention was particularly arrested by a fact trivial in itself, but in the circumstances most significant: they espied the napkin with which the head of the dead was wont to be bound not lying with the rest of the grave-clothes, but wrapped together in a place by itself.

In what garments the risen humanity of our Lord

was invested when he appeared from time to time during the forty days we are not informed, nor need we inquire; but obviously it would have been most unbecoming that he should have continued to wear the vestments of a dead man. Accordingly, before he left the tomb he divested himself of these. And is there not something which we feel to be worthy of him, though we can hardly tell why, in this little touch: that he folded up the napkin, in which his face had been enveloped by loving hands, and laid it carefully aside?

In this and in the other features of the scene St. John, with the quick discernment of love, recognized the handwriting of his Master; and there and then the truth flashed through him—"he saw and believed:" This statement appears to assign him again a priority over his companion, whom perhaps he had to instruct in the significance of the phenomena at which they were looking.

This was the most revolutionary moment of their lives, though both of them experienced other moments, both before and after, of vast importance. There, standing alone in the tomb in the morning light, they saw the glory of their Master as they had not seen it even on the Mount of Transfiguration; and they saw, in a flash, the course of their own future history. The disappointment and despair of Christ's death were transmuted, in a moment, into unspeakable joy: for they saw that their Master had not deceived them; that his death was not defeat, but a step in his triumph; and that his cause was not at an end, but only beginning. They recalled his sayings about his rising again the third day and wondered how they could have forgotten or misinterpreted them—perhaps also they began to recall some words of the Old Testament scriptures which they were afterwards to quote, with telling effect, in reference to his resurrection; for St. John expressly says that till this revolutionary moment they knew not the Scripture, that he should rise from the dead.

In great crises of experience the mind is preternaturally active and into minutes can crowd the thinking of years. Of course afterwards these thoughts were to be far more fully cleared and developed; the apostles were also to receive far more convincing evidence of the Lord's resurrection than the aspect of his empty tomb; yet it is not too much to say that, before they passed out of that rocky door, which, as they approached it, had struck into their hearts such cold and deadly terror, they were changed into new men, and had received into their souls the seeds of all which they subsequently achieved.

XXXIII.

Such was the power of the resurrection over the hearts and minds of the apostles. And it still has the same power, when it is properly realized. There is perhaps no other point in the whole circle of Christian truth to which in times of intellectual darkness inquiring spirits may so hopefully turn.

If Christ rose from the dead, then there can be no doubt that the scheme of Christianity as a whole is true. What confirmation, for example, does the resurrection lend to the miracles of Christ! This is the greatest miracle; and, if it happened, any of the rest may have happened. What a reality it imparts, too, to the world invisible, and to the life to come! If Christ rose, to begin a new stage of existence in another region of the universe, then heaven is not a dream, or a land of shadows, but actual as this earth on which we tread, and all that the Bible says about immortality receives the strongest confirmation.

The resurrection of Christ is, it is true, a stupendous event, only to be credited on the most stringent evidence. But in both quantity and quality the proof is overwhelming.

First, there is the testimony of those by whom he was seen alive after his passion. It is thus summarized by St. Paul: "He rose again the third day according to the Scriptures; and he was seen of Cephas; then of the Twelve; after that he was seen of above five hundred brethren at once, of whom the greater part remain unto this present, but some are fallen asleep; after that he was seen of James; then of all the apostles; and, last of all, he was seen of me also, as of one born out of due time." The detailed records of the Evangelists are still more impressive; and the character of the witnesses is for truthfulness above suspicion. What is said by those who disbelieve their testimony is that they were in an excited state of mind, and anxious to believe, and that their hopes created the appearances which they thought they saw. Nothing, however, is more remarkable in all the accounts than the evidence that they had no expectation whatever that he was to rise. Is it not manifest that Mary Magdalene, Peter and John had their minds preoccupied with a theory totally opposed to resurrection? Others, even after they were informed that he had risen, were thoroughly skeptical. Instead of being ready to be imposed upon by any suggestion of the fancy, they were in a state of mind to resist any evidence, however strong. Besides, what kind of fanciful appearance could have simultaneously imposed upon so many different persons in so many different places and circumstances? In their desperation to account for the facts some of the more devout believers in the literal truth of the resurrection have actually resorted to the notion that God allowed a kind of ghostly image of Jesus to appear to the different persons concerned; but surely this is more difficult to believe than the resurrection itself.

The mere testimony of those who saw the risen One is not, however, all the proof. When, immedi-

ST. JOHN AND THE RESURRECTION.

ately after the ascension, Christianity began to run its victorious course amidst the influences of Pentecost, the central theme of apostolic testimony was the resurrection; and the scene of the earliest preaching was Jerusalem. What Peter and his companions told the Jerusalemites was, that he whom they had condemned as a blasphemer and hanged on a tree had been raised up by God, who, by so exalting him, had placed on his claims the seal of heaven. This testimony brought the apostles into collision with the ecclesiastical authorities, who were concerned to repel the heresy which so discredited themselves. If Jesus had not risen, how easy it would have been to confute the preachers. The grave in which he had been laid was at hand; had the Jewish authorities been able to open the sepulchre, and show the body lying there, the apostles would have been silenced effectually and forever. Why did the authorities not do so? It will not now be said that the disciples had stolen the body.

The strongest proof of all, however, has yet to be mentioned. Convincing as the testimony of the apostles is, it is nothing at all compared with the evidence of their conduct. There cannot be a doubt that, when the Master expired and was put beneath the ground, the minds of his followers were in the lowest depths of depression and despair. They had been disappointed, if not deceived; the cause to which they had attached themselves had failed; and now all was over. They were without a head or a plan; and nothing remained for them but to return to their lowly occupations disillusioned and discredited men. Yet, a few weeks thereafter, they were before the public, full of conviction and enthusiasm, declaring that Christianity was not ended, but only beginning. What had wrought this change? It may be said, they were committed to Christianity, and could not forego the ambitions so long cherished in connection with it or return to their unexciting pursuits. The remarkable thing, however, is, that they were not now pursuing earthly ambitions; they knew they were not to gain the world, but suffer its enmity and opposition; and in point of fact they went cheerfully to prison and to death. They were transfigured men; no longer ignorant and vacillating, but wise, spiritual and determined. What had wrought this change? They say themselves that it was the resurrection; and what else could have done it? This resurrection of Christianity is a miracle in some respects more remarkable than even the resurrection of Christ; and nothing but Christ's resurrection can account for it.

ST. JOHN AT HOME AGAIN.

XXXIV.

St. John shared with the other apostles the privilege of seeing several of the appearances of the risen Lord during the forty days; but in one of them he played a conspicuous part. This took place at the Sea of Galilee, and the scene is described with great fulness in the last chapter of his own gospel.

There hangs over this story an air of mystery. Indeed, some of the details have, at first sight, the appearance of irrelevance, if not mystification. This, however, is no rare occurrence in this gospel. One of the peculiarities of St. John as a writer is that now and then he puts down, with an air of simplicity, sentences which appear to have nothing in them at all, or at all events nothing relevant to the occasion. But, as the reader, after repeated trials, is turning away in disappointment and, perhaps, a kind of resentment, suddenly, from a sharp angle of vision, something flashes out on him and, turning back, he discovers it to be a clue by which he is guided into spacious treasuries of truth, where the difficulty is not that there is no meaning, but that the meaning is too manifold.

In the present case the key seems to lie in the word "showed," which occurs twice in the opening verse—"After these things Jesus showed himself again to the disciples at the Sea of Tiberias; and on this wise showed he himself." In Greek this is a striking word, and apparently conveys more than that he made himself visible: it means that he made a fresh revelation of himself to them, showing himself in a new light or in a new character. They saw on this occasion in their risen Lord traits which were peculiarly fascinating and impressive.

One of these was a trait of tender humanity—his attachment to the scenes of his earthly experiences.

The disciples had themselves returned to Galilee from the south with a delightful sense of coming home. Probably to their provincial minds Jerusalem had always been formidable. Its pride repelled them, its Sadducean coldness and Pharisaic formalism chilled them to the bone. During their last visit this repulsion had reached a climax, for their feelings had been put under an excessive strain, and their days and nights had passed in excitement and horror. At last, indeed, a great light had burst forth upon them in the resurrection of their Lord; but as yet it was a light which dazzled even more than it cheered; and their hearts craved for solitude, that they might collect themselves and consider what was the drift of their strange experiences. Now they were back in Galilee and standing on the shore of the lake, the scene of their accustomed adventures in former days. There were the mountains and the blue waters; there were the boats and nets of their relatives, which had once been their own; the old feelings suddenly awoke in

ST. JOHN AT HOME AGAIN. 125

them, and when Peter, who felt these most keenly, said, "I go a-fishing," they were all ready to chime in, "We also go with thee." Soon they were afloat, with the sails throbbing above their heads, the water rushing beneath the keel, and the fresh breeze blowing all doubts away out of their brains.

But Jesus had preceded them to Galilee. So the angel told the holy women at the sepulchre — "Go your way, tell his disciples and Peter that he goeth before you into Galilee." This no doubt was partly due to the fact that a majority of his adherents belonged to the northern province and he intended to show himself to them alive, as he subsequently did on the mountain where he had appointed them. But there was another reason. In some respects the risen Christ was altered; the form of his humanity and the mode of his movements from place to place are enveloped in mystery. But one exceedingly human trait appears to be unmistakable: he displayed a marked predilection for the spots which had been the scenes of his former activity. To him Jerusalem had been intensely dear, whatever it was to the disciples, and he lingered in it, instructing the apostles at the very last to begin the evangelization of the world there. Bethany, where Mary, Martha and Lazarus lived, had been to him an earthly home, and he led out his disciples at the last as far as Bethany, and there he took his parting look of the world. But Galilee seems to have been the chief scene of his forty days' sojourn. It was the country of his childhood and youth; and in it had been achieved his earthly successes. The Sea of Galilee especially had been the centre of his ministry. There he had called his disciples; he had preached out of the boat on its shore; he had moved backwards and forwards from one side to another on his journeys; on its surface he had walked to the rescue of his disciples by night; within sight of it he had been followed by enthusiastic and thankful multitudes. Long it had been the focus of his thoughts and feelings; and now it draws him back.

This shows how human he was even in his resurrected state; and it brings him near to us. This clinging to the past is characteristic of human nature; however far we may wander, our hearts turn fondly to the scenes of former experiences—to the home of our childhood, to the spots where we have loved, triumphed and suffered. Few sentiments are more sacred than these; if we completely yielded to them they might bring us to Jesus.

May we not, besides, justly interpret his return to these scenes as a proof that the departed still retain an interest in the world to which they have belonged? Even the beatific vision will not blot out of the memory the charities of this earth. Heaven and earth may be far more alike than is supposed.

XXXV.

ANOTHER light in which Jesus revealed himself to the disciples on this occasion was as the Providence of their lives.

In spite of the eagerness with which they had essayed the fisherman's life again, yet that night they caught nothing. It looked as if their hands had lost their cunning. But this disappointment gave Jesus his opportunity. It was against the background of their failure that the divineness of his foresight shone out. So it is often. Many a man has been prepared for the visit of Christ by the ruin of his schemes and the break-down of his hopes. If it had always gone well with us, if the world had been entirely to our liking, and we had got everything our own way, we might never have felt any need of him. But when we had toiled all night and taken nothing, and were returning worn out and weary in the empty boat, there he was on the shore with assistance ready. And surely it is better to lose all and win him than to be so satisfied with our own success as to forget the heavenly inheritance.

As soon as Jesus took the oversight of their operations, and they cast out the net where he indicated, their labor, which had all night been so bootless, immediately became brilliantly profitable: they secured a take of a hundred and fifty and three, all large fishes; and, for all there were so many, yet was not the net broken. If God comes nigh in the crisis of disappointment, surely also he is present in the hour of success. It is through his blessing that any labor of ours is profitable. It would be a shame if it were only through privation we could be affected, and if we had no perception of the divine hand in the gifts of life.

Jesus did not, however, merely give them abundance of fish and then leave them to enjoy what they had taken. When they came ashore they found a fire with fish laid thereon, and bread. Commentators have puzzled over the question where these came from. Did angels bring them? or did Jesus create them? or did he buy them or beg them from friends on shore? What does it matter? It is enough that he provided them, as the fisherman's wife has a fire ready to warm her husband, along with the other comforts he requires, when he returns from his cold night's toil. What a practical, everyday Christ! He does not allow those who look to him to lack any good thing. He is the Saviour of the body no less than of the soul. Godliness has the promise of the life which now is, as well as of that which is to come.

He invited them to bring of the fish which they had caught, to furnish the meal more sumptuously. Then, assuming the place of entertainer, he made them all sit down and with his own hands distributed among them the blessings provided.

It is very probable that these proceedings had a special bearing on the circumstances of the disciples at the time. Long before this, when he was calling them first to be his disciples, and they were naturally troubled about where support for themselves and their families was to come from, he taught them by a similar miracle how confidently they might depend on him while engaged in his service. But at this crisis the lesson required to be taught over again. Hitherto he had himself been with them, and his popularity had insured them against want; for those who had received his miraculous aid ministered to him of their substance, and the bag which Judas carried, if seldom overflowing, was never empty. Now, however, when he was away, would not the stream of supplies run dry? Very soon they were to be sent forth to preach the gospel; and they needed the assurance that their daily bread would not fail. So Jesus had once more to show them that all the resources of the world belonged to him.

While, however, he had this special end in view, we can, besides, say in general that the *rôle* thoroughly suited him. He delighted, when in the midst of his own, to be the Entertainer. It is astonishing in his life to note how often he was present at feasting, and how frequently in his teaching he made use of images borrowed from this section of human life. "The Son of man came eating and drinking." He appreciated the uniting and sweetening power of hospitality; and he thereby left to his followers an example which they have been slow to learn. Hospitality is a Christian virtue, and it is one of the most effective modes of evangelization. Few efforts for the good of others are more fitted to be effective than when Christian men and women of standing invite to their tables the young and the humble, who see there the culture and the charm of a Christian home.

But there was more in his love of the entertainer's place. It was the expression of a nature conscious of its ability to distribute. He felt himself full of what was needed to satisfy and enrich the world. It is not for nothing that in the chief sacrament of his church he shows himself to all the ages in this character. In the Lord's Supper he is the entertainer. And whom does he invite? He follows his own maxim: "When thou makest a dinner or a supper, call not thy friends, nor thy brethren, neither thy kinsmen, nor thy rich neighbors, lest they also bid thee again, and a recompense be made thee; but when thou makest a feast, call the poor, the maimed, the lame, the blind; and thou shalt be blessed; for they cannot recompense thee." Such are his guests. "This Man receiveth sinners and eateth with them."

XXXVI.

BEFORE looking at the other ways in which Jesus revealed himself on this occasion we may pause to mark what impression he was making on the disciples. The effectiveness of a revelation depends on the apprehension of it in the minds of those to whom it is addressed, no less than on its intrinsic importance.

At first the disciples did not recognize at all with whom they had to do—"Jesus stood on the shore, but the disciples knew not that it was Jesus." It was in the grey of the morning that he appeared; and the imperfect light may have had something to do with this. But no doubt, also, their work absorbed them. Had they been assembled for prayer in an upper room, or had it been the Sabbath, they might have recognized him at once; but they did not expect him to visit them when they were engaged in business. The week-day Christ is not so easily recognized as the Sabbath-day Christ. On the sacred day we go to his house for the purpose of meeting him, and we put on our Sabbath clothes for the interview; but, if he meets us when we are in our work-a-day dress, if he is standing by while we drive our bargains, or if he comes into our homes in the hours of social mirth—and he does all these things—we are probably unprepared, and let him pass unnoticed.

In the kind question, "Children, have ye any meat?" or at least in the order to cast the net on the right side of the ship, they might surely have recognized him. But I have been told by a friend well acquainted with the sea that it is sometimes possible for one standing on the shore to detect by a peculiar ripple on the surface of the water the presence of fish at a spot where those on the water see no indication. This may have prevented them from suspecting anything more than the hint of a shrewd observer.

It was only when the miraculous haul filled the net, recalling an early experience of the same kind, that the truth flashed through the mind of St. John; and, after casting a single reassuring look landwards, he whispered to St. Peter, "It is the Lord." It only required a glance to satisfy Peter; and, hastily drawing on an upper garment, that he might not appear before the Lord in unbecoming guise, he sprang into the water and swam ashore, leaving boat, fish, comrades—everything—behind.

The entire scene is eminently characteristic. It was St. John, the man of affection and insight, who discerned Christ first; it was St. Peter, the man of passion and energy, who reached him first. Each was before the other in one respect, and both were the leaders of the rest.

It is a picture of the Church's life in all times. Believers are not all alike gifted, but all belong to the one body and are intended to serve it with their different powers. There are outstanding men needed to be leaders, and these possess diverse qualifications. Some are the eyes of the body—these are the Johns. Others are its hands and feet—these are the Peters. The highest function is that of the Johns—they are the seers, to apprehend new revelations, to point out the divine in common life, to discern the new path along which Christ is moving and calling the Church to follow. But only second in importance are the Peters—the men of enterprise and action, who advance in front of the ship and show the way. They lean on the Johns, being indebted to them for eyes, but the Johns are also dependent on them; as the national poet, who has struck out the note of liberty and made it vibrate in every heart, has to wait for the practical statesman or general who will arise to embody his dreams in deeds. Happy is the church when there are vouchsafed to her leaders of both sorts; she is happiest when she possesses them together, united in friendship as were John and Peter then, or as at the Reformation were Melancthon and Luther.

The rest of those in the boat followed, dragging the full net to the shore, where they shared the privileges of the leaders. "And none of the disciples durst ask him, Who art thou? knowing that it was the Lord." Apparently there was a difference in his appearance which might have justified such a question, but the evidence of the scene as a whole and the impression of his presence were too strong to leave room for any objections. Even Thomas, the doubter, who was one of the group of seven, was convinced.

To us, who walk by faith and not by sight, the evidence of religion can never be such as to make doubt absolutely impossible, but it is often strong enough to exclude reasonable doubt. There must be few who cannot remember some incidents in their own experience which produced an overwhelming impression of God—such as a marvellous escape from danger, or the recovery of a relative from the jaws of death, or a deliverance from what seemed a fatal business difficulty, or the unexpected opening up of a path to usefulness and honor. There are many such incidents which inevitably produce on a healthy mind the impression of a presiding Providence. Others may debate whether the thing cannot be explained by natural causes, but the man whose secret it is cannot ask: he carries it through life as a token of the divine love and care, and as often as he recalls it he says, "It is the Lord." Far stronger still, however, is the conviction springing out of a lifelong walk with Christ. Outsiders may venture to explain this away, attributing to the man's own fineness of natural disposition the holiness by which he is distinguished; but he who knows what he is in himself, and what grace has done for him, is as certain as he is of his own existence that "it is the Lord."

XXXVII.

A THIRD peculiarity of Christ revealed on this occasion was the absoluteness of his claim on the love and loyalty of his followers.

This of course came out most conspicuously in the noted scene when he thrice asked Peter, "Lovest thou me?" which, however, we must here pass by. But it came out also in a subsequent scene in which St. John was directly involved. After restoring St. Peter to his apostolic mission, Jesus said unto him, "Follow me," and apparently moved away from the rest of the group. In obedience to this command St. Peter followed, and, without receiving a command, St. John did the same. St. Peter, hearing St. John's step behind him, turned and said to Jesus, "And what shall this man do?" or, more simply, "And what of this man?"

The motive of this question has been much discussed. Some have ascribed it to irritation, as if St. Peter objected to his *tête-à-tête* with the Saviour being disturbed by the intrusion of a third party. Others have assumed the very opposite motive—that it was out of brotherly regard for St. John's welfare that he spoke. Jesus had just intimated to himself, under the veil of a figure of speech, by what death he should glorify God; and, vaguely at least, he had understood the warning. Now he asks, What of my friend: is he, too, to die the martyr's death?

That there was in the question an allusion to St.

John's future is manifest from the answer. Yet the motive was a more subtle one. The close dealing with his conscience, when Christ asked, "Lovest thou me?" had been painful in the extreme to St. Peter. Yet Jesus was now walking him away by himself; and for what purpose? Was it to press him with still more home-coming question, too sacred for the rest to hear? St. Peter was afraid of it; and this turning round to St. John, to put the question about his future, was an attempt to draw him into the colloquy; for a third in a conversation acts as screen to keep off too searching and personal topics. So he asked an idle question, apparently in anxiety about the fortunes of his friend, but really for the purpose of escaping too close contact with Jesus.

Thus almost unawares does the mind often try to avoid Christ, when he is coming near the conscience. At the well of Sychar, when our Lord was probing the conscience of the Samaritan woman, she attempted to divert the drift of the conversation by raising an ecclesiastical discussion: "Our fathers worshipped in this mountain, and ye say that Jerusalem is the place where men ought to worship." This was a subject on which logic might have been chopped forever, and during the operation what directly concerned her would have dropped out of sight. And similarly, when conversation threatens to approach personal religion, people will, if they are allowed, drift off to questions of the idly curious kind. Even in their own minds men put up such themes to shield themselves from the pressure of the claims of Christ. There are always afloat in the atmosphere of public discussion problems which can be used for this purpose. Darwinism, the Higher Criticism, Future Punishments, or the like—a man will puzzle about one of these and imagine he is studying religion, when in reality he is using his difficulties as an excuse for refusing to come to close quarters with Christ and obey the voice of the Holiest. It is possible to have a great deal to do with the outside of religion, and to enjoy religious service in which we form part of the multitude, while we carefully avoid meeting with God in secret and would dread the full light of omniscience turned upon our conduct.

In spite of St. Peter's headlong rush through the water to get to Jesus, he was far from being as confidential with him as St. John; for the close and lonely intercourse which he was shirking would have been to St. John the height of enjoyment.

XXXVIII.

On this occasion Jesus manifested his authority over his disciples, assigning to each his own work and his own destiny.

He met the idle question of the disciple with a sharp rebuke—"What is that to thee? follow thou me." He was offended at Peter's levity. The questions put to the backslider about his love ought to have driven him in upon himself and made him sober and silent; but, instead of being thus absorbed, he was starting curious inquiries about things with which he had nothing to do.

"There are two great vanities in man," says a deep student of human nature, "with respect to knowledge—the one a neglect to know what it is our duty to know, and the other a curiosity to know what it does not belong to us to know." And in no other sphere is this so true as in religion. At those solemn moments when Christ is distinctly calling and a decisive step which would change the whole course of the life is possible, how common it is, instead of replying simply and honestly, to turn round and ask, "What are others doing? what would my neighbors say?" When opportunities of usefulness arise, and Providence is inviting us to seize them, what do we say? Is it, "Here am I, send me," or is it, "What are others going to do?" In giving, for example, to schemes for the spread of the gospel, or for the amelioration of the world, how rare it is to ask simply, "What can I give? how much would God wish me to give? what ought one blessed with as much as I have been to give?" but how common to look round and ask, "What are others giving?" Thus measuring ourselves by ourselves, and comparing ourselves among ourselves, we are not wise. Our whole experience is stunted by this habit of asking what others are going to do. "What is that to thee? follow thou me."

The reference to St. John's future in the words, "If I will that he tarry till I come," may contain a hint that the apostle whom Jesus loved was to be long spared and to escape the martyrdom destined for St. Peter, but the only thing which the words expressly imply is that St. John's destiny was not the affair of St. Peter, but was taken by Jesus into his own hand.

This saying has been quoted as a proof that Jesus expected his second coming to take place soon, as his early followers expected it in their own lifetime; and it is added that events disappointed his expectation, as theirs is usually reckoned a weakness. But the weakness lies elsewhere. The attitude of the apostolic Church was the right one—the attitude of a servant on the watch, not knowing at what hour his lord may come. The date of Christ's coming depends on the faithfulness and success of the Church. So far as we are informed, he might have come even in the lifetime of his first disciples, had the faithfulness of the Church been perfect.

It is another illustration of how much easier idle curiosity is to the human mind than either accurate knowledge or plain duty that in consequence of this saying the rumor spread that St. John should not die. It not only did so at the time, but lasted long. It was said that, though buried, he was not dead, but only asleep; and St. Augustine mentions persons in his day who alleged that they had seen the earth moving above his grave. Indeed, down almost to our own time, the same superstition has reappeared every now and then in one grotesque form after another.

But the evangelist expressly emphasizes the fact that Jesus did not say he was not to die, but, "If I will that he tarry till I come, what is that to thee?"

ST. JOHN IN THE PENTECOSTAL AGE

XXXIX.

St. John's name holds a prominent place in the list of the followers of Jesus who, as we are told in the first chapter of the Book of Acts, were assembled in an upper room in Jerusalem immediately after the Ascension.

What were they doing there? They were waiting. They had been told by their departing Lord that they were to be endued with power from on high, and then their work as his witnesses would begin. What exactly this promise meant they did not know; but they were waiting to see. Already they were in possession of all the facts which were to form the theme of their testimony: they had been assured by many infallible proofs that Jesus was alive; they had seen him ascend to sit at the right hand of God; they knew that it was to be the task of their life to make these facts known. Still they lacked something. Their Master had forbidden them to appear as his witnesses till the Holy Spirit should come upon them. So they waited. They had time to think, and to arrange in their minds the remarkable experiences through which they had been passing. They had time to pray, and their prayers deepened their sense of need. The magnitude of their task expanded before their imagination, as they contemplated it; and they wondered the more what the mysterious influence was to be by which they should be qualified for executing it.

At length the hour of Providence struck, and the promise of the exalted Saviour was fulfilled, when, on the Day of Pentecost, in rushing mighty wind and tongues of fire, the Spirit descended on them. Not only was the conversion of three thousand, which immediately followed, due to this divine gift, but the whole drama of the Book of Acts—the miracles, the sermons, the extension of Christianity, the creation of institutions, the emergence of remarkable personalities, the triumph over opposition, which this book records—all are the results of the fulfilment of the promise of Christ to send the Holy Spirit. As man after man comes to the front— apostle or deacon, evangelist or prophet—one after another is described as "full of the Holy Ghost;" and this is the secret of the wonders performed. That Pentecostal age was a glorious epoch of originality, gladness and formative influence; but the inward energy by which the movement in all its developments was sustained and carried forward was the Holy Spirit.

St. John was in the very midst of these events. He, if anyone, was, in those Pentecostal days, full of the Holy Ghost. The divine power poured through him; gladness filled his heart; he was a prominent actor in all that was taking place; and he was in complete sympathy with what others were doing. His name does not, indeed, occur often, nor are there any incidents in which he is the principal figure; but the occasions on which he is mentioned are enough to give a notion of the experiences of a great time and to show that he played in it an important part.

One of the first scenes in which he is mentioned is the miraculous cure of a lame man.

St. John and St. Peter used daily to go up to the temple at the hour of prayer; and one day, as they did so, they passed a lame man, laid at the Gate Beautiful to beg for alms. The cripple was about forty years of age and had long been wont to beg there, the ugliness of his deformity contrasting with the beauty of the pillar against which he rested, and his helplessness appealing to the charity of the passers by in those moments of devotion when they were remembering their own mercies. He begged an alms of Peter and John. They happened at the time to be without money, but they were full of exultant joy; life was overflowing within them; and they were overmastered by the impulse to communicate to this helpless brother-man something of the strength with which they were blessed. In the name of Jesus Christ they commanded him to rise and walk; and immediately God fulfilled their benevolent wishes; for, the feet and ankle bones of the cripple receiving strength, he leaped up and rushed forward, holding Peter with one hand and John with the other; and he entered the temple, "walking, and leaping, and praising God."

It must have been with a strange mingling of awe and exultation that the apostles thus saw the motions of their will taking effect in the bodies of others. They knew quite well, indeed, and confessed at once, that they had not done the deed by their own power or holiness. But they were the channels through which the divine power passed; it was the Holy Spirit which both inspired them with the instinct of helpfulness and caused their philanthropic desires to take effect in this remarkable manner.

The age of such miracles is long since past. Were we, in imitation of Peter and John, to order a cripple, in the name of Christ, to rise up and walk, the physical healing would not follow. But the impulse to help is still the mark of a follower of Christ; and a sacred enthusiasm to communicate freshness and fulness of life is one of the most natural results of being filled with the Spirit of God. Nor are we without resources. We can call to our aid the skill of the medical man, the deftness of the nurse, the legislation of the statesman, the authority of the municipality, and the many other resources of science and civilization. We have to take a somewhat roundabout road, but the length of the road matters little; if only the impulse to help be passionate enough it can make long roads short. Indeed, by the use of preventive measures, by which disease and distress are cut off at their sources, Christian philanthropy is finding shorter roads than even that of miracles; and so the Lord's wonderful word is being fulfilled: "The works that I do shall ye do also; and greater works than these shall ye do."

XL.

When the cripple who had been cured went leaping and shouting into the temple, he naturally attracted a crowd, to whom St. Peter and St. John seized the opportunity of communicating the secret of the resurrection. But the temple police and some of the authorities, who chanced to be present, coming upon them, broke up the gathering and carried off the two apostles to jail as disturbers of the peace. This was the first time Peter and John had seen the inside of a prison, and it gave them a foretaste of the consequences which the new mission on which they were embarked might involve. But the heat and glow of the enthusiasm with which the Holy Spirit was inspiring them were too intense to allow them to feel such a misadventure. When, the next day, they were brought up before the Sanhedrin they not only answered the questions put to them with intrepidity, but seized the occasion to urge home on the consciences of the authorities the crime of which they had been guilty, in crucifying One of whom God had shown his approval by raising him from the dead. The force of conviction so loosed their tongues and raised them morally above their accusers that, it is said, the authorities, perceiving them to be unlearned and ignorant men, marvelled at them; and they took knowledge of them that they had been with Jesus. There are certain states of mind in which the distance put by conventional distinctions between man and man disappears, and he who has the larger manhood, or who has truth and justice on his side, towers over his opponents, who are made to feel how little the mere authority of office can avail them; and this victorious consciousness is imparted by the Holy Spirit, when it is received in purity and fulness.

Shortly after this not Peter and John only, but apparently all the apostles, were, in similar circumstances, brought into collision with the Jewish authorities. The Christian doctrine was spreading more and more; men were being converted by the thousand; and the authorities, taking alarm, cast the apostles again into prison. But they were miraculously delivered, and again appeared at their post in the temple as witnesses of the resurrection. The authorities had them brought again before their judgment-seat, but to the question why they had broken through the interdict the apostles replied that they must, in such a case, obey God rather than man. On this occasion the entire apostolic college were on the point of losing their lives, the feeling against them being so bitter that the authorities thought of stamping out the heresy by the death of all its preachers. But this murderous zeal was checked by the intervention of Gamaliel, and the feeling of the authorities was satisfied with beating the apostles and dismissing them. This, though it is so lightly told, probably means that St. John and the rest had to endure forty stripes save one—a punishment which, in ordinary circumstances, would have formed in the life of a Jew an indignity never to be forgotten. But in the state of mind in which they were it hardly made a mark on their memories, and, so far from being broken by it, "they departed from the council rejoicing that they were counted worthy to suffer shame for His name"; and they went on with their work as if nothing had happened.

A far severer trial befell St. John some time later, when his brother James was cut off by the sword of Herod. Of this incident no details are given. We do not know how James should have become a man so marked that the hand of authority struck at him in preference to any of the other apostles. But no doubt it was by the boldness of his testimony for Christ that he won this distinction; and, although the loss must have entered like iron into the soul of his sensitive brother, yet the grief of St. John would be tempered by the sense that the martyr had sacrificed his life for a great cause and had gone to inherit a great reward.

A life filled with the Holy Ghost is likely to be a life of trial and suffering, because the impetuosity of its forward movement brings it into collision with conventional authorities and vested interests; but the glow and warmth of its own feeling will lift it lightly over difficulties, and convert experiences which in ordinary circumstances would produce feelings of bitter shame and despair into reasons for joy and triumph.

XLI.

THE Pentecostal epoch was an era of marvels. The historian of it has, in every other paragraph, to remark how excitement and wonder were caused by what was happening. Not only were those astonished who saw or heard what was taking place, but the chief actors themselves were carried forward in a kind of dream of wonder, as, following the indications of Providence, they advanced from one scene of novelty to another, by a path which it would never have entered into their own hearts to tread.

Especially astonishing to them was the way in which the fences within which their religious life had been confined broke down, and they were carried into one new territory after another as preachers of Christ; the oddest circumstances sometimes giving the providential impulse to fresh developments. Not infrequently it was by persecution that the new faith was driven out of one place into another, where, but for this reason, it might never have been heard of; so that the opposition which threatened to extinguish the fire of the Gospel only scattered its embers far and wide; and wherever they fell a new fire was kindled.

Of course the supreme surprise was the admission of the Gentiles to an equal share with the Jews in the privileges of the gospel. This was one of the greatest revolutions of thought and practice in the history of humanity; but its beginnings belong rather to the life of St. Peter and its consummation to the life of St. Paul than to the history of St. John. Before, however, the decisive step was taken by the baptism of Cornelius at the hands of St. Peter, there were fragmentary and tentative movements in the same direction; and with one of these St. John had an interesting connection.

Those who were scattered abroad from Jerusalem by the persecution which ensued on the martyrdom of St. Stephen went everywhere preaching the Word; and Philip, one of the seven deacons, drifted to Samaria, where he began to make Christ known; because in those days none of Christ's followers could keep to themselves the secret which was burning in their bones. So striking were the effects of Philip's preaching that the news came to the church at Jerusalem, and St. John and St. Peter were sent down to Samaria to inspect and direct the movement.

The Samaritans were neither Jews nor Gentiles, but stood on the border line between the two; and, in ordinary circumstances, Peter and John, as strict Jews, would undoubtedly have felt scruples about holding intercourse with them. But what they saw on this occasion made them forget their prejudices; they threw themselves into the good work which was going on; they were the means of communicating to the converts the gifts of the Spirit; and, before returning to Jerusalem, they "preached the gospel in many villages of the Samaritans."

In St. John this was the more remarkable because of an incident of his earlier history which will be remembered. Being at the entrance of a Samaritan village which refused to receive his Master, he asked to be allowed to call down on it fire from heaven. Such was the natural man in St. John; such was the natural prejudice of Jew against Samaritan. But, when filled with the Holy Spirit, John was full of love, and he saw objects to admire or to pity where formerly he had only seen objects to hate and to destroy. When men are filled with the Holy Ghost they will look on their fellow-creatures with new eyes; they will see in the worst of them precious souls to be loved and redeemed. Nothing so transmutes to our feeling the most objectionable of our fellow-men as an honest effort on our part to do them good. Only get near enough any child of Adam, and there can never fail to be found in him something to which the heart can attach itself.

XLII.

One of the most remarkable features of the Pentecostal epoch was the development of brotherly feeling. The religious sentiment is a centripetal one; and, when it becomes intense, it draws men irresistibly together. Thus, in the Book of Acts, we read continually of the earliest Christians being "all with one accord in one place." They almost lived together; and for a time it looked as if they were permanently to have a common table and a common purse. In this close brotherly intercourse, it is easy to believe, the affectionate heart of St. John would take cordial part. The love of many must, however, have also concentrated itself in special friendships, and this was the case with St. John. In those days he and St. Peter became so closely associated as to be inseparable. In every scene in which St. John is mentioned in the Acts St. Peter is mentioned along with him. They were together in the upper room waiting for the gift of the Spirit; they were together when the lame man was healed; they appeared together before the Sanhedrin, and were imprisoned together; and they went down together to evangelize Samaria.

The origin of this friendship was, indeed, far earlier. John and Peter were natives of the same town. As boys they learned the same trade, and in manhood they were partners in business. They, in all probability, went together to Jerusalem to the feasts and they both were involved in the movement of the Baptist. They were introduced to Christ on the same day. Not only were both among the twelve apostles, but both belonged to the chosen Three. In many a scene of the life of Christ they were especially drawn together at the close; they exhibited their mutual understanding at the Last Supper; they were side by side in Gethsemane: they were in the high priest's palace together; and they ran together to the Lord's empty tomb. But it was after the Ascension that their friendship took its final and most perfect form. The Master whom both loved being away, each felt more than ever the need of the other. In the fire of the Pentecostal enthusiasm their hearts were riveted to each other; and thus there was formed one of the most memorable friendships of the world, like that of David and Jonathan in the Old Testament, or of Luther and Melancthon in modern times. The two men were very unlike; but this is no obstacle to friendship, but rather the reverse; for different peculiarities complement each other, if only there be a fundamental identity of sentiment; and this Peter and John had in their common devotion to Christ. What a source of happiness their friendship must have been to them, as they talked over the incidents of their extraordinary career, helping one another to recall the words of their Master and the traits of his character, and as they faced danger or labored in the Gospel, or discussed together the plans of the great enterprise in which they were engaged! Surely friendship never can be so sweet and helpful as when it is founded on common love to Christ and common enthusiasm in his work.

In this friendship St. Peter was, to outward appearance, the predominant partner. In the first half of the Book of Acts he is always the leader; and St. John retires behind his more prominent figure, playing an altogether subordinate part. But it is one of the finest peculiarities of a time like Pentecost that all engaged in the work of God forget themselves, being too concerned with the work itself to have time to spare for estimating the magnitude of their own share in it or contrasting it with that of others; and we may be certain that the heart of St. John would have been the last to envy the honor vouchsafed to another. Besides, St. Peter must have known all the time that in this friendship he was getting more than he could give. There are gifts which qualify for leadership and publicity; but those who occupy the second place, or who are hidden altogether from the eyes of the world, may have the deeper nature and the finer graces. Some gifts are intended for immediate effect; others come slowly to maturity, but their influence is far more lasting. St. Peter had the gifts necessary to break ground for Christianity, to champion it in the face of opposition and to direct its first conquests; but St. John, sunk out of sight, was far nearer the heart of Christianity. In his Gospel there is a view of the Holy Spirit widely different from that which is found in Acts. In Acts the Holy Spirit is the power by which Christianity is extended—the very power which rested supremely on St. Peter; but in the fourth

Gospel the Holy Spirit is the substitute for Jesus, the Intermediary between the invisible Christ and the visible Church, who takes of the things of Christ and shows them unto us. In the Spirit's influence, as it is represented in Acts, St. John had his share; but he especially shared in the other mode of the Spirit's influence described in his own Gospel. The things of Christ were shown to him, the character of Christ was put upon him, the spirit of Christ was breathed into him. And this gave to his fellowship a priceless value; for all other advantages which friendship can confer grow small in comparison with the charm and the influence of the beauty of holiness.

ST. JOHN IN PATMOS.

XLIII.

St. John slips, in characteristic silence, out of the Book of Acts; and the information which we obtain of his subsequent life is scanty in the extreme.

In one of St. Paul's epistles he is mentioned; and we are happy from this notice to learn that the two great teachers of Christianity met at least once face to face. Paul calls John one of the pillars of the church, the others at that time being St. Peter and St. James. This was when the headquarters of Christianity were still at Jerusalem.

In Jerusalem St. John is believed to have remained till the death of the Virgin Mary, loyally and lovingly fulfilling the charge which the Saviour had imposed on him with his dying breath. When released from this duty by her decease, he no doubt went forth like the other apostles to evangelize the world; but in what direction he turned his steps we have no information. For a considerable number of years our record of his life is an absolute blank.

There is, in one of the writings of St. Augustine, some shadow of a statement that he went to the Parthians; but it appears to be founded only on the mistranslation of a word in one of St. John's own writings. There is also a tradition of his being in Rome; and two well-known traditions are connected with this supposed residence in the eternal city. It is told that during one of the persecutions he was cast into a caldron of boiling oil, but came out unharmed; and it is also affirmed that he was given to drink a poisoned cup, but when he drank it no ill effect ensued, because the poison had taken itself away in the shape of a serpent. In mediæval art this scene is frequently represented, St. John appearing as a beautiful youth with a cup in his hand, out of which a serpent is escaping. But legends of this sort carry on their face their own refutation.

Putting such traditions aside, we have satisfactory information that he appeared in Asia Minor. This is the statement of Irenæus, who must have known the fact perfectly well, because he was a disciple of Polycarp, the martyr bishop of Hierapolis, and Polycarp was a disciple of John.

The latter part of St. John's life was spent in this region; and the city with which the unanimous tradition of early times associates him is Ephesus.

This city was situated on the Ægean coast, and it was one of the great centres of human life in that age; for Christianity, at its inception, had a predilection for large cities, whence its influence might radiate into the regions with which they were connected. Ephesus contained a great population and was a place of enormous wealth and activity. St. John may have been inspired by the aspect of its busy quays and streets when he thus described the traffic of the mystic Babylon: "The merchandise of gold, and silver, and precious stones, and of pearls, and fine linen, and purple, and silk, and scarlet, and thyine wood and all manner vessels of ivory, and all manner vessels of most precious wood, and of brass and iron and marble, and cinnamon, and odors, and ointment, and frankincense, and wine, and oil, and fine flour and wheat, and beasts, and sheep, and horses, and chariots, and slaves, and souls of men." The last awful words suggest—what was the fact—that it was an extremely wicked city. Shakespeare's account of an imaginary Ephesus, in the beginning of the *Comedy of Errors*, is too true a description of the real ancient Ephesus:

> "They say this town is full of cozenage,
> As nimble jugglers that deceive the eye,
> Dark-working sorcerers that change the mind,
> Soul-killing witches that deform the body,
> Disguised cheaters, prating mountebanks,
> And many such like liberties of sin."

Being connected by both land and sea with Syria and the countries beyond, it swarmed with those professors of black arts whom the East in that age poured in multitudes into the great cities of the West; and these preyed on the strangers from every shore who entered the harbor. The centre, however, of degradation was the temple of Diana. This was reckoned one of the seven wonders of the world. It was larger than any known structure of the kind; it had one hundred and twenty-seven pillars, each of which was the gift of a king; it contained masterpieces in both sculpture and painting of the greatest artists of antiquity, such as Phidias and Appelles; its worship was maintained by innumerable priests and priestesses; and its votaries could boast that Asia and the whole world worshipped its divinity.

Obviously this was a place where the Gospel was urgently needed; and before it was visited by St. John the work of its evangelization had been vigorously begun. It had been the chief centre of the third missionary journey of the apostle Paul, who had devoted to it three whole years. At the end of that time he was violently driven forth; but his work remained, and St. John, when he arrived, entered on the heritage left by his predecessor.

There is good reason to believe that St. Paul had not only established Christianity in Ephesus, but planted churches in the regions round about. Behind Ephesus, in the valleys of the Hermus, Cayster, and Mæander, there lay a number of important cities, such as Smyrna, Pergamos and Thyatira, Sardis, Philadelphia and Laodicea; and to these the Christian movement, if active in Ephesus, could hardly fail to penetrate. It had penetrated to them; and when St. John reached Ephesus he not only found the foundations laid in that city on which he might build, but a sphere of influence open to him in the surrounding places. This he would no doubt extend and develop, and we find him, in the opening chapters of the Book of Revelation, exercising a pastoral oversight not only over Ephesus, but also over the neighboring towns, evidently with a minute and sympathetic knowledge of the circumstances of every one of them.

XLIV.

There is only one incident of the latter half of St. John's life of which we have a complete account; and we owe the vivid picture to his own hand. It is an account of his call to be a Christian writer. A speaker for Christ he had long been; but his writing was far to exceed in importance his speaking; and he received a special call to it.

The circumstances are very fully given, and they are worthy of attention.

He was "in the isle called Patmos." This is an island at no great distance from Ephesus, one of the group, called the Sporades, scattered at this part of the coast over the surface of the Ægean. It is only a few miles in length, and is rocky and rugged in configuration; but travellers speak with enthusiasm of its beauty, when it is seen in a favorable light where it sleeps upon the lovely sea. It has a few hundred inhabitants, but it is a lonely spot.

St. John says that he was on this island "for the Word of God and the testimony of Jesus Christ;" which may only mean that he was providentially led there to receive by inspiration the Word of God and the testimony of Jesus Christ; but more probably the generally accepted interpretation is correct, that he was banished to this place for preaching God's Word and for his loyalty to Christ; because in the same breath he declares himself to be brother and companion in tribulation to those who are persecuted. Lonely islands were in that age favorite places of banishment; and Patmos may well have been used for this purpose by the authorities of Ephesus. What they intended, however, for evil turned out, through the overruling providence of God, to be for infinite good. Possibly in Ephesus St. John had been working so hard that he had little time to think and no time to write; but, when banished to this solitude, he found ample leisure. So it was when Milton's public life was violently ended by the death of Cromwell, and his outward activity limited by his blindness, that he mused the greatest epic of the world; and it is indirectly to those who kept Bunyan for twelve years in Bedford jail that we owe the Pilgrim's Progress. Prison literature has greatly enriched mankind, and at the head of all such products we must place the Book of Revelation.

Such was the place where the call came. The time was the "Lord's day." This is the only passage in Scripture where this now well-known name occurs; but, when we compare it with such a phrase as "the Lord's Supper," and when we read how the Christians came together for worship on the first day of the week, or on the same day laid by in store their gifts for poor saints, there can be no mistake to what it refers. The day of the week on which the Lord rose from the dead was already esteemed a sacred day by Christians, and in the mind of Christian Jews, like St. John, the sacredness of the Sabbath had in all probability been transferred to it.

How St. John was employed on such a day we

can without difficulty guess. He was praying, no doubt. He might be reading the Word of God. We may even make a shrewd guess at the portion of Scripture he was studying; for the Book of Revelation is steeped in the spirit and imagery of the Book of Daniel. It exhibits many traces also of another book, not in the canon of Scripture—the apocryphal Book of Enoch—and this also the apostle may have had on the island with him. He was thinking with love and intense concern of the churches under his charge, from access to which he was for the time debarred; as other exiles—Knox for example, when in Geneva, or Rutherford, when banished from Anwoth—have passionately longed for their congregations. He was thinking, too, of "the heavy and the weary weight of all this unintelligible world;" for, whether his banishment took place, as is differently reported, in the reign of Nero or in that of Domitian, it was an evil time, when the ravening wolves of persecution had been let loose and threatened to annihilate Christ's little flock.

Such was St. John's situation on the Lord's day on the lonely isle of Patmos, when his absorption deepened into the prophetic trance, or, as he puts it, he was "in the Spirit;" and then he was made acquainted with his divine vocation.

XLV.

The divine call was addressed first to the ear and then to the eye.

First, he heard behind him "a great voice, as of a trumpet." This expressed the desire of Him from whom the voice came to speak through means of the apostle: he had a message which he wished to ring like a trumpet round the world. This was further indicated by what the voice proceeded to say: "I am Alpha and Omega." These are the first and the last letters of the Greek alphabet; therefore they are the beginning and ending of all that can be written in the Greek language. And so is Christ himself the sum and substance of all which his messengers have to deliver to the world: with him they have to begin, and with him they have to end. But there could be no mistake in the interpretation of the symbol, because the voice proceeded to instruct St. John that he was to write a book, the contents of which would be divinely communicated to him, and he was ordered to send it to the churches of the province of Asia, which were under his superintendence.

So far the revelation addressed itself to the ear; but a much greater impression was produced through the avenue of the inner eye, to which there was presented nothing less than a vision of the glorified Head of the church.

Turning round to see, as he expresses it, the voice which talked with him, he saw One like unto the Son

ST. JOHN IN PATMOS.

of man in the midst of seven golden candlesticks, or rather lampstands. These candlesticks were explained to him as symbols of the seven churches of the province of Asia; and the symbolism was appropriate, for were not these churches lights shining in dark places by holding forth the illumination of divine truth? But in order to serve this purpose they required to be trimmed and supplied with oil; and this was why He whom John saw was standing or walking in the midst of them. He was watching and passing from one to another to see that their light did not go out.

Such was his work; but St. John proceeds in sublime terms to describe his aspect.

He was "clothed with a garment down to the feet, and girt about the breast with a golden girdle." The word employed for "garment" is the name for a priestly robe, so that it was in the character of priest that this superhuman Figure presented himself. Perhaps it is to the priestly character also that the next two traits apply. "His head and his hairs were white like wool, as white as snow." This has been supposed to indicate venerable age, but it is more likely that it is a symbol of priestly purity. And the other trait—"His eyes were as a flame of fire"—denotes the keenness with which he seeks for purity in others.

Two other traits appear to bring out rather his kingly character—the one, that "His feet were like fine brass," and the other, that "He had in his right hand seven stars." Feet of brass should be symbols of solid and irresistible strength, whether used for bearing weight imposed from above or for treading down opposition. There is no burden which the friends of Christ can lay upon him which he is not able to sustain; and, on the other hand, there is no force which his enemies can bring against him which he is not able to trample under foot. Woe to the opponent who feels on his neck the weight of the feet which are of fine brass! In what form the seven stars appeared in the right hand of this Figure we can only conjecture. Some have supposed them to have been set like precious stones in a ring worn on his finger or in a bracelet on his wrist, but this is perhaps too precise. These stars are afterwards described as the angels of the seven churches, by which we are to understand the authorities presiding over them. These "angels" had the churches in their hands, but they themselves were held in the right hand of Christ, as the authorities of all churches must ever be if they are to have any true success.

The two traits that have still to be mentioned may, perhaps, be said to set forth the prophetic character of Him who is here described. His voice was "as the sound of many waters." As there is no sound so mystic and subduing as the manifold voice of ocean, and as this voice murmurs upon every shore and envelops the world, so is the prophetic word of Christ intended to reach all men, and when it comes with the power of the Spirit it is irresistible. "Out of his mouth went a sharp two-edged sword"—this is the other prophetic trait. Perhaps it ought rather to be regarded as kingly, for the sword intended is that of the Judge, who will separate men at the last and recompense them according to their deeds. But it also inevitably recalls the Word of God, which is "quick and powerful, and sharper than any two-edged sword." The two meanings are not far apart, for Christ said himself in regard to everyone who heard him: "The word that I have spoken, the same shall judge him at the last day."

The final trait of the description is, "His countenance was as the sun shineth in his strength." Perhaps it ought rather to be " His aspect." It was not the face alone of this wonderful Figure, but his whole person, that emitted a dazzling light: he stood in a circle of glory; and this was as intense as the midday sun.

XLVI.

In some features of this description—especially the two-edged sword proceeding out of the mouth—we recognize the peculiarity of the Hebrew imagination, to which the harmony of one part of a picture with another was not a necessity, as it was to the mind of the Greek. Thoroughly to enjoy St. John's description we should have to translate some portions of his imagery into their Greek equivalents, so as to render the whole harmonious as a single visual perception. But there is no doubt that this is one of the most impressive visions which the Word of God contains.

What surprises us is the discrepancy between it and the Christ of St. John's memory. One would have expected that if in the vision he saw his beloved Master again the form would have been a glorified reproduction of the figure with which he had been so familiar in the days of Christ's flesh. We dare not, however, regard what he saw in Patmos merely as an image projected from his own imagination; on the contrary, it was a figure cast on the internal mirror from the outside; and the reason why it was so different from the Jesus of St. John's memory may have been because the apostle required an entirely new conception of his Master, answering to the distance to which He had removed and the state of glory into which He had entered. This may have been necessary, to impress the mind of St. John with the proper sense of His greatness.

At all events, the impression which the vision did produce was profound. As St. Paul, when the Lord Jesus appeared to him in glory on the way to Damascus, fell to the ground and was struck blind for a season, so St. John when this vision flashed upon him fell down like a dead man.

But the divine Figure at whose feet he had fallen, bending over him, touched him with his hand. This was the hand that held the seven stars, yet it could give a light and comforting touch; for, glorious and terrible as is the exalted One, yet is he that gentle Jesus who blessed the children and was the Friend of sinners. He proceeded to rally his prostrate servant with comfortable words; and then he instructed him that this vision was a divine preparation for the disclosure of the mystery which was still hidden, but which the book to be penned by him was to reveal to the world.

In many respects this experience of St. John bears a striking resemblance to the visions by which the prophetic career of Old Testament prophets, like Isaiah, Jeremiah and Ezekiel, was inaugurated. The peculiarity in this case, as has been already noted, is that the scene did not take place at the commencement of his career as a man of God, but in the middle of it, at the time when he was about to enter upon the work of a writer.

This casts an interesting light on the writings of St. John. As far as we are informed, the literary activity of no other New Testament writer was inaugurated with any such ceremony and solemnity; indeed, many of the New Testament writings rather produce the impression that their authors were unconscious of the extraordinary place to which the productions of their pens were destined. But in St. John this came to complete consciousness, and he knew when he put pen to paper that he was doing a momentous work for both God and man.

There is, however, a more general lesson: and it is one specially adapted to our own times. The prevalence of writing is one of the characteristics of the present age, and the printed page is every day becoming a greater influence in shaping the thoughts and the conduct of mankind. Through it the voice of Christ can be made to sound like a trumpet, or, like the voice of many waters, to murmur round the globe. Writing, therefore, no less than preaching, may be a service done to Christ, and it ought to be carried on with the same purity of motive and the same devotion. Nor ought the sense of responsibility to be confined to religious writing. For good or evil, no influence goes deeper than that of written words, whether they appear in letter, journal, book, or any other form; and, as in every activity of life it is the duty of a Christian man to aim at the glory of God, so in this one also ought Jesus Christ to be the Alpha and the Omega.

THE WRITINGS OF ST. JOHN.

XLVII.

THERE is no kind of influence more penetrative and enduring than that which is vouchsafed to the author who writes a book which the world will not let die; "for books are not absolutely dead things, but do contain a progeny of life in them to be as active as that soul was whose progeny they are; nay, they do preserve as in a vial the purest efficacy and extraction of that living intellect that bred them.... A good book is the precious life-blood of a master-spirit, embalmed and treasured up on purpose to a life beyond life."

When we consider how obscure was the corner in which St. John was born and how humble the calling to which he was bred, we cannot but wonder that it should have been given to him to write books which have already lasted for nearly two thousand years and yet appear to have only commenced their career of usefulness. That St. Paul, when he became a new man, should have served the cause of Christianity with his pen cannot cause any surprise, because he was an educated man: but St. John had never learned. It reminds us of the confession of John Bunyan in the beginning of his autobiography: "For my descent, it was, as is well-known by many, of a low and inconsiderable generation; my father's house being of that rank which is meanest and most despised of all the families in the land." Yet—and strange it is to think of it—among all the thousands who have been educated in our universities from century to century none have, in the charm of their style or the value of their matter, surpassed the tinker's son; of whom a critic of the rank of Coleridge has written: "I know of no book, the Bible excepted, which I, according to my judgment and experience, could so safely recommend, as teaching and enforcing the whole saving truth according to the mind that was in Christ Jesus, as the Pilgrim's Progress." The literature of Germany has a marvel somewhat similar to exhibit: Jacob Boehme was all his life nothing better than a working shoemaker, yet three hundred years after his death he can be spoken of as "the greatest of the mystics and the father of German philosophy." Philosophers like Schelling and Hegel have paid tribute to his genius, the latter calling him "a man of a mighty mind;" and a living countryman of our own says of his writings: "I wade in and in, to the utmost of my ability, and still there rise up above me and stretch out around me and sink down beneath me vast reaches of revelation and speculation, attainment and experience, before which I can only wonder and worship.... Boehme, almost more than any other man whatsoever, is carried up till he moves like a holy angel or a glorified saint among things unseen and eternal. He is of the race of the seers, and he stands out a very prince among them. He is full of eyes, and all his eyes are full of light."

Examples like these remind us that there is no

rank of life so lowly or corner of the world so obscure as to be inaccessible to the light of the glorious mystery of existence. No mind and no lot need be commonplace, if only the heart be opened to the beauty and the truth with which it is surrounded. Among the poor, if this awakening comes at all, it generally is due to the touch of religion. And, as regards St. John, it was obviously by the influence of Christ that his sensibilities were quickened, and it was by the exigencies of the work of Christ, in which he was engaged, that his slumbering powers were called into exercise.

In his writings there are manifest traces of the unlearned man. More than once he betrays his impatience in the use of "paper and ink," like one unaccustomed to composition. The Greek of his earliest book is decidedly peculiar; and, although his prolonged residence in Ephesus improved his language, he avoids even in his latest writings all the complexities of literary style, having formed for himself a dialect of extreme simplicity. Yet through the imperfections of his language the originality and majesty of his thoughts do not fail to find a way. The ancient Church called him the eagle, meaning that among the writers of the Bible he is the one who soars highest and is able to gaze most steadily upon the sun of truth. They called him also Epistethius, the Recumbent One; meaning that, not only once or twice, but always he was lying on the bosom of Jesus and listening to the beating of His heart. To St. John Jesus Christ was the Truth, eternal and absolute, issuing from the Father to be the Light of the world; and in this sunlight John lived continually. But at the same time Christ was the Love, infinite and absolute, in contact with which the apostle's heart was filled with satisfaction and ever fresh desire. And, as Truth and Love in one, He was to him the Life eternal. It was by this unwearied intuition of Christ and by absorbing love to him that St. John was made a writer; for in writing, as elsewhere,

> "It is the heart, and not the brain,
> That to the highest doth attain;
> And he who followeth love's behest
> Far exceedeth all the rest."

XLVIII.

The writings of St. John belong to three species: one is an Apocalypse, one is a Gospel, and three are Letters.

Although the Book of Revelation stands last in the Bible it is undoubtedly the first of St. John's writings. This is indicated in the book itself, in the beginning of which he gives an account of his call to the work of authorship; and there are many other indications of the same thing. The book exhibits the apostle's mind at an early stage of development, when it was furnished with materials of which it was subsequently to a large extent displenished. Indeed, so vast is the contrast between the storm and stress with which this book is filled and the serenity of St. John's later writings that it has been doubted by many whether they can have proceeded from the same mind. But the providential experiences through which St. John lived were of a very revolutionary order, and his was a nature capable of passing from extreme excitement to supreme tranquillity.

The mind of the writer of the Book of Revelation is dominated by two events of the most agitating import—the Neronian Persecution and the Fall of Jerusalem.

The first heathen persecution of Christianity took place at Rome at the hands of the Emperor Nero, and it was of a terrible description. The Christians were accused of setting fire to the city and thus causing a calamity which had inspired the inhabitants with bewildering terror. Popular feeling was thus let loose against the obscure foreign sect, and the wildest excesses of cruelty were perpetrated. Many were thrown to wild beasts in the amphitheatre, and others were enclosed in sacks full of pitch and, being stuck on poles, were burned to illuminate the gardens opened by the Emperor to appease his excited subjects. Some suppose that St. John was in Rome at the time and witnessed these atrocities; but, whether he was or not, it is easy to understand what an effect they must have produced on his sensitive heart; and the mental excitement into which he was thrown deeply colored his writing in Revelation.

The other influence under which he wrote was the emotion caused by the approaching fall of Jerusalem. The Jews had attempted to throw off the yoke of their Roman masters, who thereupon advanced against them with irresistible force, for the purpose of crushing the Jewish state out of existence. From province to province and town to town the destruction swept, till Jerusalem was girdled round with the besieging army; and the city fell after months of suffering, during which scenes of horror and carnage had been enacted such as humanity has hardly ever witnessed elsewhere. This took place in the year 70 A. D., and St. John's book was probably writen a year or two earlier.

It is in form an Apocalypse—a literary form at that time greatly cultivated among the Jews. One book of the Old Testament—the prophecy of Daniel—

is written in it; but in the period between the Old Testament and the New many books of this species appeared, the most notable of them being the Book of Enoch, which still survives. As the name implies, an Apocalypse is a disclosure of the secret purposes of God. In the fifth chapter of Revelation a book is seen in heaven sealed with seven seals, which none in heaven or earth can open; but the Lion of the Tribe of Judah prevails to open the book and to loose the seals thereof. This is the Book of fate, or rather of Providence; and, as seal after seal is broken, the secrets of Providence are successively made known. After the seven seals ensues the blowing of seven trumpets, with a similar import, and this is succeeded by the pouring out of seven vials, in the same sense. The disclosures made by the seven seals, the seven trumpets and the seven vials form the body of the book. The whole is extremely obscure, and, as is well-known, no portion of Scripture has given rise to such diversity of interpretation, some interpreting it as referring to the events then happening in St. John's own experience, others as descriptive of the entire course of human history from that date onwards, and still others as giving information of what will happen at the end of the world.

It is possible that the author was compelled to be obscure; because, if he had expressed his ideas in plain language, he would have exposed both himself and his fellow-Christians to the persecuting rage of the Roman government, which extended also to Ephesus, where he was. If, for instance, the Beast to which he refers as the supreme enemy of the Church be, as many suppose, the Emperor Nero, it is obvious that he could only have referred to him in terms carefully veiled.

Bewilderingly obscure, however, as many chapters of the Revelation are, no book has ever more fully served its purpose. This is to prove that there is a Providence in human affairs which is on the side of righteousness, and, in spite of the opposition of the infernal and bestial elements in the world, will secure the final triumh of Christianity. This great lesson can be read on every page; in periods of persecution the book has always been a consolation to the Church, and it will always have an office to fulfil. Of course there are other passages, such as the Epistles to the Seven Churches, the teaching of which is perfectly plain; and to this book the world is largely indebted for the imagery in which it conceives the Christian heaven.

XLIX.

Of St. John's later writings we do not know for certain which was first, but probably it was his Gospel. A whole generation had intervened between his first book and his second, and in the interval he had greatly changed. The atmosphere of the Gospel is quite different from that of the Revelation. The Fall of Jerusalem had happened in the meantime, and this had created a revolution in the minds of Christians. It proclaimed with the irresistible voice of destiny that the old dispensation, with its temple, rites and limitations, had passed away, and that a new era had dawned upon the world. It cut Jewish Christians loose from a thousand prepossessions and caused them to realize how free and universal a thing Christianity was to be. In the Book of Revelation St. John is still entangled in Jewish imagery, hopes, claims, and -modes of thought, but in the Gospel he has moved out into the wide and sunny ocean of humanity.

It is said that in the old age of the apostle the presbyters of Ephesus begged him to commit to writing his recollections of his Master, lest the precious treasures of his memory, by which they had often profited, should be lost. Nothing could be more probable than this, but tradition has added, in its exaggerative way, that he thereupon at once, in an access of inspiration, began to recite the opening verses of his Gospel—"In the beginning was the Word, and the Word was with God, and the Word was God." This reminds me of a picture of St. John I have seen, from the pencil of one of the old masters, in which he is represented as having just written these words, when he pauses and lays down the pen, gazing awestruck at the characters which express a meaning far beyond his own power of comprehension.

The Gospels of St. Matthew, St. Mark, and St. Luke were, of course, by this time in existence, and probably they were well known both to the apostle and his fellow presbyters; but his reminiscences covered different grounds from theirs. This was one reason for which he wrote—to supplement their information. He passes over many things narrated by them, though he takes them for granted, and, indeed, his narrative but seldom runs parallel with theirs. It is from him we learn that the public ministry of Christ lasted for three years, whereas from the Synoptists we should have inferred that it lasted but one. The reason is that they confine themselves, except at the last, to the Lord's movements in Galilee, whereas St. John narrates in great detail His visits to Jerusalem, which they have omitted. They describe his life in public, his miracles, his parables to the multitude; he commemorates his interviews with individuals. The Synoptists supply the exterior life of Christ, St. John the interior.

There must, in the nature of things, have been a Christ different from the one seen by the multitude, and St. John, by the make of his mind and the course

THE WRITINGS OF ST. JOHN. 179

of his experience, was the man to delineate this hidden Christ. He had been with him oftener than any other; he had caught shades of his meaning which others had missed; he treasured his rarest and most private sayings.

In St. John Jesus not only draws upon a larger circle of ideas than in the Synoptists, but speaks with a different accent; and the question has often been asked whether He is not made to speak with the Johannine accent. Here and there, after reporting a speech of his Master, the evangelist goes on to write down reflections of his own, without indicating where Christ's words cease and his own begin. Is this an indication that he knows his own ideas to be so completely identical with Christ's, and due to Christ, that he did not feel the necessity of distinguishing exactly between what he remembered and what he himself had thought?

The picture of Socrates presented in the Dialogues of Plato differs from the biography of him given by Xenophon in a manner not unlike the way in which the discourses in St. John differ from those of the Synoptists. Plato idealized his master, being conscious that his own thoughts were a legitimate development from those of Socrates. Perhaps, to some extent, the same may have been the case with St. John; but, if so, the freedom with which he acted was due to the certainty of his own inspiration.

In his lifetime Jesus had said: "I have yet many things to say unto you, but ye cannot bear them now;

howbeit, when he, the Spirit of truth, is come, he will guide you into all truth." And St. John was so satisfied that this had been fulfilled in his experience that he could freely give the sense of his Master without painful scrupulosity about its form.

L.

There was probably also another reason for the writing of St. John's Gospel. It is well known that we owe the most of the writings of St. Paul indirectly to the false teachers with whom he had to contend; because they provoked him by their opposition and false accusations, and he blazed forth against them with fiery and irresistible statements of the truth. At the time the necessity was grievous to him, but the work has reaped from it unspeakable advantage. The discussions and the heresies of St. Paul's day had been left behind by the time St. John wrote his Gospel, but others had arisen in their stead. From his epistles we learn that his righteous soul, too, was vexed with false teachers, who endeavored to entice his converts away from the truth. These are generally understood to have been the precursors of those who were known later as Gnostics; and the drifts of their speculations was to obscure either the true divinity or the true humanity of Christ, while in practice they warped the plain rules of righteousness and purity.

If St. John wrote his Gospel with such opponents before his eyes, there may have been for him and his first readers in many a verse a peculiar emphasis which is now lost to us. This may especially have been the case with the great verse in which he explains the purpose of his writings: " These are written, that ye might believe that Jesus was the Christ, the Son of God; and

that, believing, ye might have life through his name."
His purpose was to prove, first, that Jesus was the
Christ—that is, that he was the Heir and the Fulfiller
of the Old Testament. Although St. John was by this
time liberated from the Jewish prepossessions, the Old
Testament was still for him a divine revelation and the
ancient history a preparation for the Messiah. But, in
order to sustain the office of Messiah, Jesus had to be far
more than those supposed who had on their lips the
name of the Messiah they were expecting: to sustain the
mighty load of human salvation only one Being in the
universe was sufficient; and therefore God "gave his
only begotten Son." The second thing which St. John
wrote his Gospel to prove was that Jesus is the Son of
God. This truth is not peculiar to him, nor was it
first made known in his Gospel. It is the common
faith of all the writers of the New Testament. It un-
derlies the testimony of the Synoptists; St. Paul glories
in it; the author of the Epistle to the Hebrews states
it explicitly. But St. John was able to bear more emphatic and authoritative witness to it than any other
figure of the apostolic age; and this he does especially
in his Gospel. "We beheld his glory," he says in the
prologue, "the glory of the Only Begotten of the Father, full of grace and truth;" and the whole book is
an endeavor to let others see what he had seen. It
is a succession of unveilings of the glory of the Only
Begotten. He does not make use of all his materials.
For example, he only gives seven miracles; but these
are chosen as typical and conclusive. The whole book
is a cumulative proof that Jesus was the Son of God.

THE WRITINGS OF ST. JOHN.

Yet St. John's aim is not merely theoretical: there is an ulterior object, expressed in the words, "and that, believing, ye might have life through his name." He meant his readers not only to assent to the demonstration of Christ's claims, but to receive him as their life. And the whole story is so told as to show how those who received him for what he claimed to be were blessed with eternal life, while those who did not receive him were more and more hardened in their sin, until their guilt culminated in the murder of the Prince of Life.

LI.

Of the epistolary species of writing we possess three specimens from the pen of St. John.

Two of these, his second and third Epistles, are simply short private letters, which have fortunately been rescued from oblivion to give a vivid glimpse into the life of that distant age as it was being formed by Christianity.

One of them is addressed to a person styled "the elect lady," or, as it may be translated, "the lady Electa" or "the elect Kyria." St. John had met some of her children at the house of a sister of hers, and, finding them to be decided Christians, he writes to the mother a few warm words of congratulation, taking advantage of the opportunity at the same time to warn her against the abuse of her Christian hospitality by wandering teachers who were not genuine servants of Christ. One of the features of early Christianity was the number of refined and high-toned women who found in it satisfaction for the aspirations of the heart. It is easy to understand how an aged saint with the qualities of St. John should have been a friend and confidant in homes over which such women presided. His interest in the young people is extremely noticeable and characteristic; for he speaks with warmth not only of the children of the lady to whom he writes, but also of the children of her sister, with whom he was staying.

The other little note is addressed to a gentleman; and its purpose is to commend to his attention certain evangelists who were about to visit the town in which he resided. It reminds us of St. Paul's brief Epistle to Philemon; and, like it, supplies a specimen of apostolic courtesy, as well as a glimpse of the changes which Christianity was introducing into the social relationships.

The remaining letter, St. John's first Epistle, is of quite a different character. It is not long, but it is more a short treatise than a letter in the common acceptation of the term. It has not, like St. Paul's epistles, a superscription designating the writer and the recipients. It has been suggested that it was written at the same time as the Gospel and intended to accompany it as an *envoi*, and this notion has a great deal to recommend it. For instance, the opening words, "That which was from the beginning, which we have heard, which we have seen with our eyes, which we have looked upon and our hands have handled of the Word of life," are far liker a description of the Gospel than of the contents of the Epistle which follows. The whole composition would serve admirably as a companion-piece to the Gospel, to explain its drift and enforce the practical objects for which it was written.

It exhibits the apostle's leading ideas more clearly, perhaps, than even the Gospel; at least it does so in a space so narrow that they cannot be overlooked. St. John has not, like St. Paul, long arguments and doctrinal statements, but he has watchwords which he is constantly repeating. Truth, light, life, love—these are to him the priceless possessions. They are all in God. Here we find again and again the statement, "God is love," the greatest sentence which man ever uttered. All these possessions, however, and God himself, are brought nigh to men in Christ, and it is by abiding in him that we enjoy them. In this blessedness St. John had lived for a lifetime, and the purpose of his writings was that others might have fellowship in the same blessedness.

Perhaps, however, the chief purpose of the Epistle is to be found in the many earnest exhortations it contains in reference to the behavior of those who profess to belong to Christ—not to sin, but to keep his commandments; not to yield to the enticements of the world or to fear its hatred; to love the brethren and take advantage of every opportunity of doing them good. "He that saith he abideth in Him ought himself so to walk even as He walked."

ST. JOHN THE BAPTIST.

ST. JOHN THE BAPTIST.

CHAPTER I.

BIRTH AND UPBRINGING.

Luke 1: 5-80

THE birth of the Baptist is woven along with that of Jesus into one exquisite story, in which we learn how his father, when offering incense in the temple, was informed, through an apparition of the angel Gabriel, of the approaching event, but was struck dumb for his unbelief; how the virgin Mary, after being informed by the same angel of her impending destiny, paid a lengthened visit to her cousin Elizabeth on the eve of the Baptist's birth, and the two holy women affectionately greeted each other; and how, at the circumcising of the child, the tongue of the father was loosed, so that he was able to tell the name which his son was to bear, and at the same time to break forth into a hymn of praise for the honor conferred on his family.

Great difficulties have been felt by Christian scholars about this story, but these are considerably relieved when we perceive the truths which it embodies.

The first of these is that the Baptist's was a predestined life.

It was to emphasize this fact that the element of

miracle was allowed to enter so largely into the circumstances of his birth. When events take place in the ordinary course of nature we are apt to overlook their significance; and hence it has seemed meet to the Creator sometimes to accompany his working with circumstances so unusual as to arouse attention and make the truth so plain as to be unmistakable.

The parents were old and had ceased to have the hope of children. In similar circumstances, the "father of the faithful," in times remote, received the promise of a son; and the special favor of God, thus indicated, heightened his sense of gratitude and strained his anticipations to the utmost as to the issues bound up in his son's life. Zacharias and Elizabeth, in like manner, must have felt that their child was in a peculiar way a gift of God, and that a special importance was to attach to his life. When anything has been long desired, but hope of ever obtaining it has died out of the heart, and yet, after all, it is given, the gift appears infinitely greater than it would have done if received at the time when it was expected. The real reason, however, why in this case the gift was withheld so long was that the hour of Providence had not come. The fulness of time when the Messiah should appear, and therefore when his forerunner should come into the world, was settled in the divine plan and could not be altered by an hour. Therefore had Zacharias and his wife to wait.

As a rule, the naming of children takes place in haphazard fashion, the child receiving a certain name simply because some relative has borne it before him or because the sound has pleased the fancy of father or mother, or for some similar reason. But on this occasion the name was divinely decided beforehand; and this was another indication that this child was created for a special purpose. The name John signifies The Lord is favorable, or, put more briefly, The Gift of God. He was a gift to his parents, but also to far wider circles—to his country and to mankind.

Not only was this child to be a gift, but he was to be gifted; so the father was informed: "He shall be great in the sight of the Lord." To be a great man is the ambition of every child of Adam; and the thought of having as a son one who is a great man is a suggestion which thrills every parent's heart. Greatness is, indeed, an ambiguous word. Who is great? To be notorious, to be much in the mouths of men, to have a name which is a household word—that is the superficial conception of greatness. But such greatness may be very paltry; to as much greatness as this multitudes of the meanest and most worthless of mankind have attained. But John was to be great "in the sight of the Lord." This is a different matter: it implies not only genuine gifts, but gifts employed for other than selfish ends.

Not only, however, was it indicated in general that this child was to be a great man; but the special task was specified in which his gifts were to be employed. He was to be a prophet: "He shall be filled with the Holy Ghost from his mother's womb, and many of the children of Israel will he turn to the Lord their God." To be a prophet had in that country long been the height of human ambition. Yet even this was not the summit of the honor intended for the son of Zacharias. An honor far above what any prophet of the Old Testament—even an Elijah or Isaiah—had attained was to be vouchsafed to him: to be the forerunner; going before the Messiah to prepare his way.

If this was really the destiny of John it will not appear very surprising that it should have been miraculously revealed beforehand. Yet perhaps the chief lesson which we have to learn from the miracle is not that the birth of John was exceptional, but rather that every birth is more wonderful than we are apt to suppose. God saw fit to accompany his working in some cases with miracle, making his meaning unmistakable, in order that we might learn to take his meaning always. Every life is predestinated. It is not by chance that anyone is born at a particular time and in a particular place. In the period which his life covers and in the place where his lot is cast everyone has an appointed work to do and a place to fill in the divine plan; and his gifts are measured out by the divine hand to enable him to fulfill his destiny. "In my cradle," said a great poet of our own century, "lay the map of my line of march, marked out for my whole life."

But, if this be so, what becomes of human freedom? it may be asked. And this objection has actually been urged against this story. If, it is said, God knew beforehand what John's course in the world was to be John could not have been a free agent. But this difficulty will not dismay us. It is only by means of human coöperation that the divine purpose in any life

BIRTH AND UPBRINGING.

can be fulfilled. Anyone also may frustrate the grace of God. Multitudes do so—and not seldom the most gifted. The light of genius is to them a light that leads astray; their talents are misspent, and become a curse instead of a blessing: and they will appear before the judgment-seat with the work undone for which they were created. It is just such a great life as John's which brings home to the mind the full extent of this danger. What if he had failed? What if, yielding to the passions of youth or the temptations of the world, he had quenched the Spirit and, instead of being a prophet, to lead his fellowmen up to God, had been a ringleader in evil, using the force and fascination of his genius to lead men down the broad road! Is it conceivable that he was never tempted? that he never stood trembling at the parting of the ways? Is it credible that the preacher of repentance did not know the fascination of sin? No man attains to a life of honor and usefulness without passing through the crisis of decision and fighting many a battle with the world, the flesh, and the devil. It may not matter so much to the world whether or not our life fails; but it matters as much to ourselves, for it is the loss of the one chance of living, and it is an eternal loss.

Another lesson which is charmingly taught by this story is that there are good people in the worst of times.

It is in the cycle of stories with which the birth of Christ is surrounded—and along with them we reckon the incidents connected with the birth of the

Baptist—that we obtain by far the most vivid glimpses of the best section of Jewish society in that age—*die Stillen im Lande*, who were waiting for the consolation of Israel. Indeed, without this portion of the evangelic records we should have hardly any clear information about these hidden ones and their state of mind. Yet they were essential to the rise and spread of Christianity; and, now that we have the records, we can see that they describe them exactly as they must have been.

It was an evil time. The people of God had sunk very low both in character and in fortune. It was the darkest hour, which occurs just before the dawning. The nation was enslaved to the Roman power; and its own princes, of dubious origin, were the exact reverse of the ideals of the nation's prime. The Pharisee and the Sadducee occupied the high places of religion—the one as scribe, ruling in the synagogue, the other as priest, ruling in the temple. Life on the outside was thickly plastered over with pious rules and practices, but on the inside it was full of dead men's bones. The publican, the sinner and the harlot flaunted their vices in the eyes of all; and the bitter critics of these abandoned classes practised the same sins in their hearts.

Even as one reads the body of the Gospels, the impression one receives is that, till Christ came and converted a few, piety was extinct. But this impression is corrected by these stories of the childhood of Jesus. As in the days of Elijah, when the great prophet complained that he was left alone in the land, his countrymen having in a body gone over to idolatry, God was able to inform him that there were seven thousand in Israel who had not bowed the knee to Baal, so in this dark age there were scattered saints in every part of the land—Elizabeths, Josephs, Marys, Simeons, Annas—who were keeping the fire of true religion unextinguished. Even in the temple—the focus of evil—a man was to be found like Zacharias, who when he had come up to Jerusalem in the order of his course to fulfil the order of his priesthood, and when he was chosen by lot to burn incense—the sign that the prayers of Israel were ascending to heaven at the hour of prayer—did not merely perform the ceremony, but accompanied the mechanical act with such fervent intercessions that an archangel was attracted from heaven to assure him that his prayers were heard.

In the hymn of Mary, when she greeted Elizabeth, and in the hymn of Zacharias, when his tongue was loosed on the occasion of his child's circumcision, we are enabled to see into the very hearts of all who were of their way of thinking and to recover the contents of their minds.

The most prominent feature was an intense patriotism. They dwelt on the memories of their country's glorious past, and into their very souls had entered the iron of its dishonor: but, above all, they fed their hopes on the promises given to Abraham and to David which still awaited their fulfilment. Combined with this was an intense love for the Holy Scriptures. In them they were brought into contact with the godly figures of the past ages, in communion with whom they found the companionship which the degenerate generation by which they were surrounded did not afford. The hymns of Mary and Zacharias are saturated with the spirit and the language of the lyrics of the Old Testament. And, along with devotion to the Scriptures, another prominent feature of the piety of these people was prayer. Assured that God's promise could not fail they ardently pleaded for the dawn of a better day, and especially for the advent of the Messiah. When Gabriel announced to Zacharias that his prayer was heard, it is generally supposed he meant his prayer for a son. But for such a gift Zacharies had long ceased to plead: it was for the coming of the Messiah he had been praying; and this was the prayer of all like-minded people. Thinly scattered throughout the population they yet knew one another, and, as occasion allowed, blew into flame the fire of hope and devotion in one another's hearts. They were for the most part poor and obscure, like Joseph the carpenter or the shepherds of Bethlehem; but they looked for changes which would reverse the judgments of the world by which they were condemned to neglect and contempt. Thus did Mary sing, "He hath put down the mighty from their seats, and exalted them of low degree; He hath filled the hungry with good things, and the rich he hath sent empty away."

Not only are there good people in the worst of times, but to them, however few and humble they may be, the future belongs. Principalities and powers may lord it over them; wickedness in high places may be contemptuous; the notorieties of the hour may dazzle them down; but those in whose hearts and in whose homes the altar-fire of truth, righteousness and piety is kept burning are the true kings, and their hour will come. Some day there will pass through their ranks from mouth to mouth the cry, "To us a Child is born, to us a Son is given, and the government shall be upon His shoulder." In these stories of the childhood of Jesus we see how, in a moment, the sadness of those who were clinging to principle and waiting for the kingdom of God can be turned into joy, and their silence and sighing become hymns of praise. From Mary to Zacharias, from the shepherds to Simeon and Anna, the inspiration passed; and their closed lips were opened to hail the good time that had come. And this is a prophecy of that which will happen to all who live in the same attitude; for "light is sown for the righteous and gladness for the upright in heart."

A third lesson which is taught by the story of the Baptist's birth and upbringing is the influence of parents.

It has been already said that the Baptist might himself have frustrated the purpose of God in his life. In order that the divine plan might be fulfilled it was necessary that his own mind and will should rise into harmony and co-operation with it. But it was also dependent on the sympathy and the efforts of his parents. Had they not appreciated the design of God in their son's life, and brought him up with this in view, all might have been lost.

The character of Zacharias and Elizabeth is described in attractive terms: "They were both righteous before God, walking in all the commandments and ordinances of the Lord blameless." The father was a priest, and so there was an atmosphere of religion in the home. But this may not always be an advantage. Where religion is a man's occupation there must be the form of godliness; but this may only make the contrast the more glaring between profession and practice. The eyes of the young are quick to detect such inconsistencies; and perhaps the most dangerous position in which a young and observant boy can grow up is a home where religion is a trade, but not a life. That incident in the temple, however, already referred to, proves that Zacharias' religion had an inside as well as an outside. When he was offering incense, he was at the same time offering what the incense symbolized—fervent prayer. Besides, the hymn of the father and the greeting of the mother to Mary show that both were acquainted with the poetry of religion. Their religion was a faithful discharge of duty; but it was not all duty; it was a passion and an enthusiasm as well. It is said of them both that they were filled with the Holy Ghost. This is the kind of religion that wins young hearts—where they see that it is not a yoke, but the secret of blessedness. It was of special significance that in this home both parents were godly. The mother had not to weep because the boy's father was thwarting her teaching by his example, nor the father to sigh that the mother's unsanctified nature was hardening his son. Then, there would be the more distant influence of relatives and acquaintances of like spirit with the father and mother; for we may be certain that the friends of this family would be the excellent of the earth.

Happy is he or she who has such a father and mother, and whose childhood is nurtured in such a home. Out of such homes have come the men who have been the reformative and regenerative forces of the world. The influence of the mother is especially noteworthy; nearly all men who have been conspicuously great and good have owed much to their mothers. In this narrative the mother is less prominent than the father; but enough is told to show what manner of spirit she was of. One likes to think of the three months spent by Mary under her roof. The homage paid by Elizabeth to her on whom had been bestowed the greater honor of being the mother of the Lord was an anticipation of the humility of her son, when he said, "He must increase, but I must decrease."

Their home is said to have been "in a city of Judah," which some have proposed to read "the city of Juttah," a priestly town to the south of Jerusalem. Others have thought of Hebron, another priestly town in the same region. But it is useless to attempt any determination of the exact place.

Whatever the town was, here "he grew and waxed strong in spirit, and was in the deserts till the day of his showing unto Israel." He was not an educated man in the technical sense. He did not go to Jerusalem and sit at the feet of Gamaliel. He was self-taught, as the saying is; perhaps in this case we ought rather to say God-taught. It is curious to note how many of the world's greatest men have owed nothing to schools and colleges. Universities can polish the intellect, but can they add to its primordial mass? When the mass of intellect is great, sometimes it is all the more impressive and effective for not being polished too much. The Baptist's discourses show that he was not ignorant of the world; so that we must not understand too literally the statement that he was in the deserts. But, if he visited towns and there observed human life, and if he visited Jerusalem and there scrutinized the state of religion, he retired to the deserts to brood over what he had seen. He brooded long. It does not appear that his ministry began much before that of Jesus; and, as Jesus was thirty years old when He went forth to preach, John must have been about the same age when he was shown unto Israel. All this time his thoughts had been accumulating; deeper and deeper, as he wandered brooding among the solitudes, grew his convictions, " as streams their channels deeper wear." At last he came forth, clothed with a force like that of the bare elements of nature, and speaking with the impressiveness of the thunder and the vividness of the lightning.

On the title page of this volume a sentence is quoted, from one of Mrs. Jameson's books on Sacred Art, to the effect that " in devotional pictures we often see St. John the Evangelist and St. John the Baptist standing together, one on each side of Christ." To what link of association is this conjunction due? The identity of name may have something to do with it.

Besides, the two were at least distantly connected by the tie of nature; for the Baptist's mother is called "the cousin"—a vague word in Greek—of Mary, the mother of Jesus, and, as the Evangelist's mother was in all probability Mary's sister, it is likely that the Evangelist was related to the Baptist in the same way as Jesus was. But the tie which binds the two together in the Christian mind is rather that indicated by the words, "One on each side of Christ." The two St. Johns form the extreme links of the chain of evangelic testimony. The Baptist had the privilege of being the first to point out the Messiah; the Evangelist bore the last and most consummate witness to the glory of the Son of God.

CHAPTER II.

THE PROPHET.

Matthew 3 : 1-12; Mark 1 :1-8; Luke 3 : 1-18.

SOME preachers derive a certain amount of influence from the impression made by their personal appearance. When, as in the case of Chalmers, on the broad and ample forehead there rests the air of philosophic thought, and in the liquid eye there shines the sympathy of a benevolent nature, the goodwill of the congregation is conciliated before a word is uttered. Still more fascinating is the impression when, as in the case of Newman, the stern and emaciated figure suggests the secret fasts and midnight vigils of one who dwells in a hidden world, out of which he comes with a divine message to his followers.

In the highest degree this advantage attached to the preaching of the Baptist, whose appearance must have been very striking. His hair was long and unkempt; and his features were tanned with the sun and the air of the desert. Probably they were thinned too by austerity; for his habitual food was of the simplest order, consisting only of locusts and wild honey. Locusts, dried and preserved, form still, at the present day, an article of food in the East, but only among the very poor: people in the least degree luxurious or scrupulous would not look at it. Wild honey, formed by hives of bees in the crevices of rocks or in rifted trees, abounds in the desert-places of Palestine, and may be gathered by anyone who wanders there. The raiment of the Baptist corresponded with his food, consisting of a garment of the very coarsest and cheapest cloth, made of camel's hair. The girdle of the Oriental is an article of clothing on which a great deal of taste and expense is laid out, being frequently of fine material and gay coloring, with the added adornment of elaborate needlework; but the girdle with which John's garment was confined was no more than a rough band of leather. Everything, in short, about his external appearance denoted one who had reduced the claims of the body to the lowest possible terms, that he might devote himself entirely to the life of the spirit.

John was a Nazarite. The Nazarite vow seems to have been of very ancient origin, perhaps having existed earlier than the beginning of the history of the Hebrew people. But it was adopted into the Mosaic legislation. It was voluntary; and it was usually temporary. For ascetic purposes an Israelite might resolve to be for a certain term of months or years a Nazarite, and at the end of this period he could, by the performance of certain ceremonies, lay the ascetic habit aside and return to ordinary life. The Baptist, however, was, like some other great men of his race, such as Samuel and Samson, a Nazarite for life. The vow consisted in letting the hair grow uncut and in abstinence from the fruit of the vine in every shape and form. The object of it was to subdue the bodily appetites and to cultivate an unworldly life in fellowship with God.

Among the learned there has been much discussion

as to whether the Baptist, besides being a Nazarite, was an Essene. The Essenes are named by Josephus and other ancient writers along with the Pharisees and Sadducees as a third school of religious thought among the Jews, but they are never mentioned in the New Testament. They were ascetics, who fled from the world and lived as a separate community in the same desert of Judah in which John spent his days before his appearance to Israel. It has even been disputed whether Jesus did not belong to them and owe to them some of his doctrines. But Christianity is fundamentally opposed to Essenism in the high regard it pays to the body, and in its doctrine that the religious life is to be lived not out of the world but in it. John's teaching, too, is widely separated from the false unworldliness of the Essenes, though in some respects his manner of life resembled theirs. The most curious point of agreement is that the highest object of Essene aspiration was to attain to the spirit of Elijah. Now, John in some respects strikingly resembled Elijah. Not only did his external appearance recall that ancient prophet, who is expressly described, in 2 Kings 1:8, as "a hairy man, and girt with a girdle of leather about his loins," but the angel who foretold his birth stated that he would be clothed with the spirit and power of Elijah. The Baptist's relations to Herod and Herodias were closely parallel to those of Elijah to Ahab and Jezebel; and the suddenness with which he burst into view out of the desert in which he had spent his youth recalled the great prophet who, from his solitary cell on Mount Carmel, used to descend to beard the monarch in his palace or to challenge the assembled nation to choose between Jehovah and Baal. Our Lord himself taught that in the Baptist Elijah had returned to rouse and warn the people of God.

The audiences of different preachers vary exceedingly. They vary in size. Some preachers, even when they are appreciated, preach to a handful; others draw the million. They vary in quality. Some preachers appeal only to a single class, it may be to the cultivated, their words being "caviare to the general," or it may be to the common people, their manner offending the fastidious; but the greatest preachers draw all classes.

John did so emphatically. Jerusalem and all Judæa went out to him. No sooner did his voice sound in the desert than an electric thrill seemed to pass through the country; there arose a rumor and a fame, and the population streamed out *en masse* to hear him. The Pharisee, ever intent on examining any new phenomenon appearing in the religious world, was there as a matter of course; but so was the Sadducee, whose cold soul was usually inaccessible to religious excitement. The scribe was there, to hear what new doctrine the famous preacher would produce from the Scriptures, which were the subject of his own study; but the publican and the harlot were also there, who in general cared nothing for Scriptures or doctrines. Even soldiers are mentioned as among John's auditors, though whether these were Roman or Jewish is uncertain.

The scene of the ministry to which this motley multitude flocked was the valley of the Jordan. Different points of the valley are mentioned by different Evangelists, from the desert of Judah on the south to the ford of Bethabara, just below the Sea of Galilee, on the north. These differences as to locality have been treated as discrepancies; but surely without reason. A preacher would naturally move from place to place, and be sometimes on one side of the river and sometimes on the other. The slight indications which are supplied in the Gospels seem to show that John moved, on the whole, from south to north, beginning in the south, near his home, and ending in the north, near the abode of Herod, by whom his career was stopped.

It is especially worthy of note that the population " went out " to John. He did not go to them—to their cities, their synagogues or their temple. The idea of our modern Home Mission movement is to carry the Gospel to the people—to the lanes and courts of the city, to the miner's hut and the fisherman's resort, to the man on the street and the woman in the house—so that they cannot get away from it; and we speak fervently of our methods as aggressive. But it should not be forgotten that there is another method—the attractive. Speak the right word, and you will not need to press men to come and hear it. The spiritual instincts of human nature may be dormant, but they are not dead. Let the right music sound outside, and the hidden man of the heart will rise and come to the window to look out and listen. No obstacles can keep people away when a voice sufficiently charged with the Holy Ghost is heard. John had only to lift up his voice, and the entire country hastened to hear him.

THE PROPHET.

The message of this preacher was exceedingly simple. It contained only two watchwords, the one being "Repent," the other, "The kingdom of heaven is at hand."

Repentance is perhaps not the best rendering of the first note of John's message; conversion would be a more literal translation. It was for an entire change in the habits of thought and conduct that John called; and this change included not only the forsaking of sin but the seeking of God. Still, the forsaking of sin was very prominent in John's demands; for we are told how pointedly he referred to the favorite sins of different classes. When the publicans asked, "What shall we do?" he had his answer ready, "Exact no more than that which is appointed you;" unjust and vexatious exactions being notoriously the sin of this class. So, when the soldiers demanded, "What shall we do?" he pointed his finger straight at their besetting sins, when he said, "Do violence to no man, neither accuse any falsely, and be content with your wages." The boldness of such preaching is manifest: the last mentioned word, for instance, "Be content with your wages," was probably no more popular then than it would be if preached to the poor at the present day. But, if John preached fearlessly to the poor, he had a no less practical message to the rich; for to them he said, "He that hath two coats, let him impart to him that hath none; and he that hath meat, let him do likewise." It is extraordinary how evil habit can, generation after generation, override the most elementary instincts of justice and humanity. The average conduct of both the masses and the classes is at the present day in many respects just as distorted as it was in the days of the Baptist. But the true prophet is he who can see how far the line of custom diverges from the line of righteousness and can summon forth the conscience of every man to acknowledge it too.

The other note of John's preaching was the kingdom of God. This was not a novel watchward. The ideal of the Jews had always been a theocracy. When Saul, their first king, was appointed, the prophet Samuel condemned the act of the people as a lapse: they ought to have wished no king but God. And when, in subsequent ages, the kings of the land with rare exceptions turned out miserable failures, the better and deeper spirits always sighed for a reign of God, which would ensure national prosperity. The deeper the nation sank the more passionate grew this aspiration; and when the good time coming was thought of, it was always in the form of a kingdom of God. It is, indeed, a point which has been much discussed, how far such hopes were prevalent immediately before the Advent. But the New Testament itself proves incontestably that the expectation of the Messianic king was one of the principal features of the deep and hidden piety of the land, while Messianic hopes of a totally different order, crude and earthly, were widely diffused among the people. At all events, in the Jewish mind there was latent a whole system of Messianic ideas, which only a hint was required to awaken into activity.

It was to this that John appealed when he cried,

"The kingdom of God is at hand." But his most effective word was the hint that not only the kingdom but the King was coming. His favorite way of characterizing himself was "as the voice of one crying in the wilderness, 'Prepare ye the way of the Lord.'" In the East, when a king was making a progress through any part of his dominions, a herald preceded him, to announce his approach and to clear the way. If no road existed one had to be made, valleys being filled up and even mountains and hills levelled for the purpose. Every obstacle, in short, had to be removed, and the hearts of men prepared for the king's reception. Such was the office which John claimed to fill in the programme of the Messianic King.

The two portions of John's message—repentance and the kingdom of God—were closely connected: he called on men to repent that they might be ready for the King when he came. Indeed, here was the very point of the Baptist's preaching. He was profoundly convinced that his countrymen were not prepared, and that no kingdom of God could be formed out of them as they were. They, indeed, had no idea of this themselves; but this ignorance was the supreme obstacle. They imagined that, simply because they were children of Abraham, they could go in a body into the kingdom; but he cried; "Begin not to say within yourselves, We have Abraham to our father." Children of Abraham! rather, I should say, children of the old serpent are ye—"O generation of vipers." The King, when he came, would not admit them, as a matter of course, into his kingdom: on the contrary, the very first thing he would do would be to sit as a judge, to separate the good from the evil. "His fan is in his hand, and he will throughly purge his floor, and will gather the wheat into his garner, but will burn up the chaff with unquenchable fire." This "wrath to come" must be the first act of the Messiah's activity. John, therefore, called upon men at once to be converted, that they might be considered meet to enter into the kingdom when Messiah came. Words and professions would be of no avail— " Bring forth fruits meet for repentance."

Is it not obvious that this is a message for all time? In one sense the Baptist's ministry was an evanescent one: when Christ came, there was no place for him any more. But in another sense the Baptist is always needed. Christ comes to many; but he receives no welcome because they feel no need of him. Unless a man knows that he is lost, the announcement of a Saviour has no attraction for his mind. The deeper the sense of sin, the firmer the grasp of salvation. In the kingdom of God the hungry are filled with good things, but the rich are sent empty away.

The prophets of Israel were poets as well as preachers; and one way in which they displayed their poetical endowment was by the invention of physical symbols to represent the truths which they also expressed in words. Thus, it will be remembered, Jeremiah at one period went about Jerusalem wearing a yoke on his shoulders, in order to impress on his

THE PROPHET.

fellow-citizens the certainty that they were to become subject to the Babylonian power; and similar symbolical actions of other prophets will occur to every Bible reader. In the Baptist, ancient prophecy, after centuries of silence, had come to life again; and he demonstrated that he was the true heir of men like Isaiah and Jeremiah by the exercise also of this poetical gift. He embodied his teaching not only in words, but in an expressive symbol. And never was symbol more felicitously chosen; for baptism exactly expressed the main drift of his teaching.

Perhaps in the invention of this symbol John was not altogether original. The truth is, washing with water is so natural and beautiful a symbol of spiritual cleansing and renewal that it has been used by religious teachers as an initiatory rite in all ages and in all parts of the world. It is said to have been in use in the Holy Land before the age of the Baptist as part of the ceremonial by which a heathen was made a proselyte of the Jewish faith. If this be correct, the fact lends to John's adoption of the rite peculiar significance. His countrymen were already familiar with the notion that a heathen, in order to be admitted to a place among the people of God, had to undergo a change which baptism symbolized: he had to wash away his old sins; he had, in fact, to die to his old life, and to become a new creature. But it had never before occurred to them that they themselves, the seed of Abraham, required any such transformation before entering the kingdom of the Messiah. When, therefore, John called upon them to submit to baptism he was teaching the same lesson as our Lord taught Nicodemus when he said, "Except a man be born again he cannot see the kingdom of God."

Another important end which baptism served in the ministry of John was that it brought his hearers to decision, and was a means by which they made confession. Under the preaching of the Word impressions are often made by which the heart is melted and the whole being thrown into a state of aspiration; but, because nothing is done to bring the mind to a point, emotion cools down, ordinary motives resume their sway, and nothing comes of the impressions. It is well known how missions and revival preachers try to obviate this risk by inquiry meetings, testimony meetings, and the like; and, though such methods may be abused, they have their value. The most august method of the kind is participation in the Lord's Supper. This sacrament is, like the baptism of John, a symbol of truth; but it is also a means of bringing those who have been impressed with the truth to the point of confessing Christ. And, if John's call impressed the honest and good hearts among his auditors when he urged them to come forward, in the eyes of all, and submit themselves to the rite of baptism, surely the voice of Jesus Christ should move us far more when he says, "Do this in remembrance of me."

CHAPTER III.

THE BAPTISM OF JESUS.

Matthew 3:13-17; Mark 1:9-11; Luke 3:21, 22.

The multitudes were baptized of John in Jordan, "confessing their sins." His preaching of the terrors of the law revealed the secrets of men's hearts to themselves, and they were glad, by the word of confession, to exorcise what they felt to be condemning them. Many a confession he heard from lips which had never been opened to confess before; and the sad and bad secrets were made known to him of many a life which in the eyes of the world looked spotless. In such a situation he must have learned to know the weaknesses of the human heart; and it would not surprise him to hear that there were guilty memories gnawing and tormenting many a breast in which the world would never have expected them.

But one day there appeared among the applicants for the baptismal rite One who, at the first glance, he was so certain had no sin to confess that he drew back and said, "I have need to be baptized of Thee, and comest Thou to me?" In other cases John may have refused to administer the rite because repentance was not deep enough; in this case he refused because repentance was unnecessary. The task of John was to bring sin home to the consciences of men; but here was One who brought it home to his own conscience.

As he looked on Jesus, the baptizer felt that he himself needed to be baptized; as, in comparison with dazzling whiteness, even some kinds of white look grey. John was the boldest of men: Pharisee or priest, soldier or king could not make him quail: but he quailed before this Applicant who sought the benefit of his office.

If John knew Jesus before this there is nothing surprising in the scene. But John is made by one of the Evangelists to state that till this day he had not known Jesus. It has been argued, indeed, that this may only mean that he did not, before he saw the signs vouchsafed on this occasion, know him as he really was—as the Messiah. He must have known him, it is held, as a man, because their families were closely related; and, although the one family lived in Galilee and the other in Judæa, they had opportunities of seeing one another at the feasts in Jerusalem, which both families were sure to attend. These seem cogent arguments; but there may have been many reasons, to us unknown, for their never having seen one another before this day; and the unsocial habits of John, reaching back we know not how far into his early life, suggest a reason which may have been sufficient to keep them apart.

If John never saw Jesus before, the impression made on his mind and conscience by this first encounter is a striking revelation of the character of Jesus. There are rare faces which in some degree make the same impression. There sits on them an air of purity and peace, which, without words, tell its story—the story of a hidden life spent in walking with God—and many people would confess that they have been made more sensible of the coarseness of the fibre of their own nature and the raggedness of their own conduct by being brought casually face to face with such a breathing image of goodness than by the exposure of the most subtle moral analysis or the denunciations of a hundred sermons. In the life of Christ there are numerous instances of the overwhelming effect which the mere aspect of his personality in some of its moods was able to produce. It will be remembered how in the boat St. Peter fell down before him and, grovelling, cried, "Depart from me, for I am a sinful man, O Lord;" how on the last journey to Jerusalem he went on in front of the Twelve and "they were amazed, and as they followed, they were afraid;" and how in Gethsemane the soldiers sent to apprehend him, when they beheld him, started back and fell on their faces to the earth. There can be no doubt that when Jesus came to the baptism of John he was in a state of unusual exaltation, for he was on the eve of entering upon his public work, and this rapt state of mind may have communicated to his appearance an unusual impressiveness; so that, even before ascertaining who he was, John recoiled with a religious dread, as in the presence of a superior being. As in his mother's womb the babe leaped when the Lord drew near, so now an overpowering instinct impelled him to draw back from assuming towards him a position which seemed to be that of a superior.

The first meeting of these two is a unique scene.

They were of nearly the same age; they were related according to the flesh; they were both men of prophetic endowment, sent to produce in their native country a religious reformation. Yet, in spite of these and other points of resemblance, there could not have been two characters more absolutely contrasted. Jesus marked the contrast in the broadest way when he subsequently said, "John the Baptist came neither eating bread nor drinking wine; and ye say, He hath a devil: the Son of man is come eating and drinking, and ye say, Behold a gluttonous man and a winebibber, a friend of publicans and sinners." John was the child of the desert, courting solitude and avoiding human society; Jesus followed a homely trade, appeared at marriages and feasts, was a friend of women and children, and was as much at home in the busy city as on the mountain top. John called the multitude out to the desert to hear him and did not condescend to visit the haunts of men; Jesus went to sinners where he could find them, considering it his duty to seek as well as to save that which was lost. John has a seared look; he is a man who, after severe struggles, has obtained the mastery of himself and is holding down a coarse nature by main force; Jesus, on the contrary, is always innocent and spontaneous, genial and serene. John, in short, is the Old Testament personified, Jesus the embodiment of the New; and in John's shrinking from baptizing Jesus the spirit of the Old Testament—the spirit of law, wrath and austerity—was doing homage to the spirit of the New Testament—the spirit of freedom and of love.

THE BAPTISM OF JESUS.

The application by Jesus for baptism perplexed John; and we must confess it perplexes us. It is not, indeed, entirely without parallel in the life of Christ; for his circumcision, which took place when he was eight days old, raises the same difficulty. The difficulty is, that he should have participated in an ordinance which symbolized the removal of sin. But in this case it is more urgent, because he made the application himself.

Did this betray a consciousness of sin? Such was the meaning of the application when made by others; and certainly this would be the natural construction to put on the conduct of Jesus, if it were not at variance with everything else we know about him. The sinlessness of Jesus is one of the truths to which the Scripture bears the clearest testimony; and it has been believed in by many who have not accepted the testimony of Scripture about him in some other respects. He claimed himself to be without sin; and in the accounts which have come down to us of his prayers there does not occur a single syllable of confession. This is justly accounted one of the most remarkable features of his life. Other religious characters have confessed their own sins; and the profounder their holiness the more frequent and piercing have been their professions. But Jesus, confessedly the most profoundly religious figure that has appeared in human history, made no such acknowledgements. Why? Was this a defect in his religious character, or was the reason, that he had no sin to confess? So the Scriptures say. Not only is the image of Jesus which they present one which breathes out purity from every feature, but they expressly assert, in many different forms of statement, that he was holy and harmless and undefiled and separate from sinners. Even on this occasion the impression which he made on John was that he had no need of baptism to take away sin; and his own statement, "Thus it becometh us to fulfil all righteousness," seems to imply that up to this point he was conscious of perfectly fulfilling the divine law. Therefore, his application cannot be explained as evidence that he was conscious of sin.

What, then, is the explanation? Why did one who had no sin seek to participate in an ordinance which was expressly called the baptism of repentance? It is by no means easy to answer.

It has often been asserted that the explanation is given in the reply of Jesus to John, "Suffer it to be so now; for thus it becometh us to fulfil all righteousness." But these words only inform us that he felt it to be his duty to take part in the ordinance; they do not tell us why he considered it obligatory.

Some have dismissed the difficulty by saying that it was a marvellous instance of the Saviour's humility, that he, the sinless One, should submit to an ordinance intended for sinners. And they have added poetic reflections to the effect that, while the water cleansed others, he cleansed the water, and so on. But this is no explanation. Neither is the suggestion satisfactory, that he took part in it to encourage others. John's baptism, it is said, was a great religious movement; and Jesus, as a religious character, could not keep out of it. He countenanced all religious services, and was so strict in his attention to those of the synagogue and the temple as to recall to the minds of onlookers the saying, "The zeal of thine house hath eaten me up." Now, it is true that Christ did give an ever-memorable example of conscientiousness in attendance upon religious services; and this habit may be included in the "all righteousness" which it had ever been his desire to fulfil. But this would not account for, or even justify, his participation in an ordinance which had no meaning for himself. It might account for his baptizing, but not for his being baptized.

Only two explanations seem really to touch the quick. The one is that John's baptism had a positive as well as a negative side. It was not only the baptism of repentance, but a rite of dedication. It was a renewal of the national covenant, the inauguration of a new era, the gateway of the kingdom of God. Now, although Jesus had no part in the sin from which baptism cleansed, he had part in this positive enthusiasm: he was the very person to lead the way into the new era. The other explanation, which may very easily be combined with this one, is that he received baptism as a representative person. Although sinless himself, he was a member of a sinful nation, of whose sin he was keenly conscious—more so than any other whom John baptized—and he went along with the rest of the nation in making confession. In short, he was in this act rehearsing beforehand the great act of his death, when he bore in his own body on the tree the sins of the world.

John may not as yet have understood why Jesus wished to be baptized; but, with the same reverence with which he had shrunk from administering the rite, he yielded when Jesus repeated his request.

The manner in which this mysterious candidate received the rite must still further have heightened John's respect and awe. St. Luke informs us that Jesus came up from the water praying. This is a solemn hint as to the spirit in which all divine ordinances ought to be received. When we come to the font seeking baptism either for ourselves or others, when we sit at the Lord's Table, when we are on our way to church, when we open God's holy word— as we take part in every such ordinance—we may learn from Jesus how to conduct ourselves: the best state of mind is, to be engaged in prayer.

What may we suppose he was praying for? If we remember the nature of the ordinance in which he was participating and the stage of his own development which he had reached, can we doubt that he was praying for the coming of the kingdom of God and for strength to play his own part in its inauguration?

The answer to his prayer came suddenly and impressively. While he was yet speaking his Father in heaven heard, and three wonders happened: first, the heavens were opened; secondly, the Holy Spirit, in the form of a dove, descended on him; and, thirdly, a voice came from heaven, saying, "This is my beloved Son, in whom I am well pleased."

THE BAPTISM OF JESUS.

At this point many questions arise. First, what is meant by the heavens opening? The language used in the Evangelists is very graphic, suggesting that the appearance occurred of a rent being made in the blue vault, by which the invisible things which lie within were disclosed. But what does this mean to us, who are well aware that the visible heaven is not what it was thought to be by the infant mind of the race—the floor of a celestial palace, the occupants and furnishings of which might be seen if an opening were made in the ceiling of our earthly abode?

Then, what was the dove which descended on Jesus? Was there a real dove, which, attracted by his gentleness, alighted on him, as such creatures, when domesticated, will sometimes do on persons to whom they are drawn by kindness and amiability? Or was the dove a form of light which glided, with dove-like motion, down on his head, to point him out, as at Saul's conversion a light above the brightness of the sun shone round about him? An ancient legend says that the whole valley of the Jordan was illuminated. And what was the voice? Was it thunder, which in Scripture is frequently called the voice of God? There were other scenes in the life of Christ when divine voices from heaven were heard for his benefit, and on at least one of these occasions the bystanders heard thunder and nothing more, whilst in the ears of those more directly concerned the sound shaped itself into an articulate divine-message; and it seems a reasonable inference that the other divine voices—the present one among them—were of the same description.

This raises the question whether the multitude, on this occasion, or only Jesus and John, heard the divine voice. Some devout interpreters have held that all three signs took place in the consciousness of Jesus and John alone, and had no place in the world of the senses. But judgments on such a point are largely subjective, and it is not for one Christian to impose his opinions on another.

At all events, the signs were of divine origin; and both to Jesus and John they were of the utmost value.

For Jesus this was a transfiguring moment—one of the cardinal points in the development of his humanity, marking his transition from the life of a private man to the career of a public teacher. Some suppose that it was at this point he became fully conscious of his unique relationship to God and grasped in all its majesty the plan of his subsequent career. There is more unanimity in the belief that it was now he was endowed with the miraculous powers of which he was to make use in his ministry. In the gospels his miracles are ascribed to the Holy Spirit. This does not mean that his own divine power was not at work in them, but that his human nature required to be potentiated by special gifts of the Holy Spirit, in order to be a fit organ through which his divinity might act. And perhaps it was at this time that these gifts were conferred. Such questions belong, however, rather to the life of Christ; and at present we are concerned with the life of the Baptist.

THE BAPTISM OF JESUS.

To John this was a moment big with destiny. Before this, in his secret intercourse with God—but at what exact date and in what exact manner we know not—he had received a premonition to this effect: "Upon whom thou shalt see the Spirit descending, and remaining on him, the same is he which baptizeth with the Holy Ghost." This, then, was the sign for which he had been waiting; this was the day for which he had been born. The appearance of the sign was the assurance that all the revelations of his desert experience and all the words he had ventured to utter in the name of God were true. The new era which he had announced was no mirage which would disappear, as the visions of enthusiasts have often done. Here, under his very eyes and in his very hands, was the King, to whom it belonged to set up and to establish the kingdom of God.

CHAPTER IV.

HIS TESTIMONY TO CHRIST.

John 1:19-37; 3:25-36.

The culmination of the Baptist's personal experience was reached when, standing in the water of Jordan, he saw and heard the signs with which the baptism of Jesus was accompanied. But still he had a great work to do in bearing testimony to the Messiah. There are three recorded occasions on which he did so : the first when a deputation was sent to him from Jerusalem by the ecclesiastical authorities; the second when he pointed Jesus out to his own disciples as the Messiah;' and the third when he rebuked the attempt of his disciples to stir up rivalry between Jesus and himself. And on each of these occasions John not only bore conscious witness to Christ, but at the same time unconsciously revealed his own character.

There are three names applied by John to Christ, in which his testimony is summed up, and which may be taken as clews to this part of his life—the Son of God, the Lamb of God, the Bridegroom.

It was entirely proper that the ecclesiastical authorities at Jerusalem should send a deputation to ask the Baptist who he was. They asked first if he was the Messiah, then if he was Elijah; then if he was "that prophet," meaning probably by this term the great prophet whose coming was predicted by Moses in the famous words of Deut. 18 : 15: "The Lord God shall raise up unto thee a prophet, from the midst of thy brethren, like unto me; unto him ye shall hearken."

It may surprise us that to the question whether he were Elijah he answered No, when on the Holy Mount our Lord identified him with that prophet: "But I say unto you that Elias is come already, and they have done unto him whatsoever they listed." But John and Jesus used the name in different senses. Besides, John might be Elijah without knowing it. His distinguishing grace was humility; he did not know how great he was; 'he wist not that his face shone;" he did not dare to identify himself with one held in such supreme estimation as Elijah. When asked to say what he was, he would only say, "I am a voice"—the nearest thing to nothing. A voice may, indeed, produce momentous effects, if it sounds at the right moment; and John hoped to do so; but as a voice dies on the air and is forgotten, so he expected to pass out of sight and out of mind.

Observing his lowly estimate of himself, we are rather surprised to notice the credit given him for not claiming to be the Messiah—"He confessed," says St. John, "and denied not, but confessed, I am not the Christ"—as if he might have done otherwise, or had been tempted to do so. Was he ever thus tempted? There seems to be no doubt that there existed in the masses of the people plenty of latent Messianic expectation; and one who had made an impression so profound could easily have set on fire this combustible material. Some of John's adherents may have hoped that he would do so. Perhaps also there may have been a time when he had not yet become conscious of the limits of his own commission—before he was specifically informed of the part he was to play as the forerunner of Him who was to come. But if ever any such ambitious ideas had harbored in his mind or been pressed upon him by others, he was able at the proper moment to divest himself of them; and at last he trampled them beneath his feet.

"I am not the Christ," he said with decision; "but," he added, "there standeth One among you whom ye know not;" and then he reverted to a figure of speech often employed in his earlier ministry, and touchingly expressive of the lowly estimate he had formed of his relation to the Messiah. His shoes, he said, he was unable to bear, and his shoe-latchet he was unworthy to unloose. To bear the shoes of a person or unloose his shoe-latchet was among the humblest offices performed by slaves; and thus John protested that he was not worthy to be even the slave of the Messiah.

On some occasions, when he made use of this comparison to designate his own insignificance and Christ's superiority, he added words which showed how well he knew wherein the difference between them lay: "I," he said, "baptize with water, but he will baptize with the Holy Ghost and with fire." He felt that his own work was superficial, external, cold: it was only baptism with water. But there are defilements which cannot be removed with water. The ore, for example, in which metals are embedded has to be cast into the furnace that the dross and dirt may be removed with fire and the silver or gold come forth pure. And equally searching is the purification required by human souls. It is not enough to break off notorious sins, as John commanded his hearers to do; there must be kindled in the heart the love of God and the enthusiasm of humanity. John's work was negative; but it required as its completement a positive work—to create in the heart from which sin had been expelled the passion for goodness. In short, in addition to the baptism of water, John knew there was needed the baptism of fire; and he was well aware he had not this to give.

This gift which John possessed, of seeing over and beyond his own work, is one of the most remarkable; and can only be found where there exist a rare self-knowledge and a rare humility. To the worker his own work is usually ultimate; it reaches as far as the horizon and up to the zenith; and this is all the more likely to be the case the more earnest is the man. The evangelist, for example, thinks that the great work of the Church is conversion, and he has little conception of the importance of the slow formation of character; the pastor, on the other hand, who has watched over the young of his congregation and instilled into their minds the principles of the gospel, may find it hard to realize that they still require a complete change of heart. But John not only acknowledged that his own work was merely a commencement, but saw with perfect clearness what was needed to make it complete.

This invested with special significance the sign by which Jesus was marked out in his baptism; for the sign was the descent on him of the Holy Ghost. "God giveth not the Spirit by measure unto him," said John on a subsequent occasion. With this divine fire he was not only filled, but it overflowed for the baptism of the world.

On one occasion, referring to this descent of the Spirit on Christ, John said, "And I saw, and bare record that this is the Son of God." This is John's first great name for the Saviour; but what he intended by it has been the subject of frequent discussion. It is a name which in different parts of Scripture has different meanings. In the Old Testament, where it is applied to kings and to the nation of Israel as a whole, it means the favorite of God; probably in Christ's time it had come to be a popular name for the Messiah; and in the documents of Christianity it has the highest meaning of all, designating the unique relationship of Jesus to God. At which precise stage of the history of this idea the Baptist grasped it is a fair subject for discussion. It is not to be forgotten that John borrowed the name from the voice from heaven which sounded at the baptism of Jesus. Probably it meant for him all that he himself had not but Jesus had—all that was required to finish the work which he had begun but was not able to complete.

It may have been while Jesus was away in the wilderness, into which he plunged immediately after his baptism, to endure the forty days' temptation, that the deputation from Jerusalem came to John; and it has been supposed that it was immediately after Jesus returned from the wilderness, the temptation being finished, that John pointed him out to his own followers as the Messiah. It is easy to conceive that, after so unique and prolonged an experience as Jesus had passed through in the wilderness, there may have been in his aspect something unusually impressive; and, when he came suddenly again into the circle where the Baptist was standing, the first look at him sent through the forerunner's soul a revealing shock; whereupon, with outstretched finger pointed to him, he cried, "Behold the Lamb of God, that taketh away the sin of the world."

What was the nature of the impression which had been made on John's mind by the aspect of Jesus and drew forth this exclamation has been a question much discussed. Some suppose that it was by the meekness and gentleness of Jesus he was impressed; and that there flashed through his mind the pictures of the twenty-third Psalm, in which the happiness of a soul at peace with God is set forth under the image of a sheep or lamb in its relations with the shepherd. Many have supposed the reference to be to the suffering servant of the Lord in the fifty-third of Isaiah, "led as a lamb to the slaughter." The tense look of Christ, possessed with the purpose of his life, had instantly suggested to John how much he was likely to suffer in conflict with the "generation of vipers," to which he had himself appealed in vain. Many have supposed the reference to be to the paschal lamb or other lambs of sacrifice. By a sudden inspiration John was enabled, it is supposed, to anticipate Christ's sacrificial death. In favor of this is recalled the fact that he was of priestly descent, and familiar, through his father, if not through his own experience, with all kinds of sacrifice.

Possibly in the impression flashed into John's mind by the aspect of Jesus there was something of all these thoughts—of Christ's lamb-like innocence and faith, of his high-strung devotion likely to come into painful collision with a coarse world, and of his death for the world's sin. John had predicted that Jesus would baptize with fire—that is, that he would fill his adherents with holy passion and enthusiasm. But how was he to do this? He would baptize them with the Holy Ghost. But the Holy Ghost is not a physical influence: he works through ideas and emotions. Where, then, were the ideas and emotions to come from? We know where, historically, they have come from. They have come from the cross of Christ. It has been by the sight of Christ giving himself for them that human hearts have been inspired with hatred of sin, with the passion for holiness, with self-sacrifice and missionary zeal. This is the Lamb of God that has, in fact, taken away the sin of the world; and the likelihood is that it was this Lamb of God that John, though perhaps through a glass, darkly, foresaw.

On this occasion also John's testimony to Jesus was accompanied with an unconscious revelation of his own character. After one day saying, "Behold the Lamb of God," to his followers in general, he said it another day to two of them in particular, who inter-

THE TESTIMONY TO CHRIST. 231

preted it as a direction to them to leave their master and follow a new one. So John intended it. He freely gave away these two disciples—two of the best, for one of them was St. John, afterwards the Evangelist—and others followed. It was a hardship to part from such dear friends and companions; but he deliberately brought the magnet into operation which, he knew, would draw with an irresistible attraction; for the best hearts about him were, through the influence of his ministry, pining for the baptism of fire which Christ was to impart.

The third occasion when John bore conspicuous testimony to Christ was when "there arose a question between some of John's disciples and the Jews about purifying." In the revised version this incident is given more correctly: "there arose a question on the part of John's disciples with a Jew about purifying." Who this Jew was and what was his motive, we are not informed. The "purifying," however, about which he and they disputed would appear to have been nothing else than baptism. Jesus, it seems, had followed the example of John by baptizing for a time, "though Jesus himself baptized not, but his disciples." And the new attraction proved more potent than the old, the fickle crowd leaving John and flocking to the baptism of his successor. If, as is likely, Jesus had begun to preach as well as baptize, it is easy to understand how his voice, with its gracious words, dulled the impression even of John's eloquence. Possibly the Jew was one who had been baptized by Jesus, and the disciples of

John fell into dispute with him as to whether the baptism of Christ was superior to their master's. Or perhaps he was a mischief-maker, who thought he could set the two parties by the ears; and he commenced with casting up to John's disciples that their master was being deserted, because the crowd was flocking elsewhere.

If this was his intention, he was only too successful. There is an unmistakable tone of irritation in the words in which John is addressed by his disciples: "Rabbi, he that was with thee beyond Jordan, to whom thou barest witness, behold, the same baptizeth, and all men come to him." The suggestion was that Jesus had kicked away the ladder by which he had risen, and that his success was at the expense of his friend.

It was such a speech as would have played havoc with a little mind and an unprincipled soul. Never are the suggestions of self-love so dangerous as when they are whispered in the ear by the flattering lips of sympathizers. When thoughts of envy arise within our own breasts we can more easily recognize their true character; but when they are suggested by friends they have a deceptive air of impartiality, and we think we can trust the estimates of outsiders. Many a man not destitute of either greatness or goodness has been filled with peevishness and self-pity, and even with furious jealousy and resentment, by just such suggestions from his friends or family as were made to John by his disciples.

The situation, was, indeed, a trying one. There are few experiences more dangerous to the vanity of

HIS TESTIMONY TO CHRIST.

human nature than such a position as John had attained, with its fame and rumor, its crowds, its excitement, its success; there are few heads which such an experience will not turn. But, if the tide of popularity ebbs as suddenly as it has risen, or goes away to another candidate for public attention, the situation is still more testing; in such circumstances the heart of many a public favorite has broken. When for a lifetime a man has stood on the pinnacle of influence, but at last his day is over and another appears to take his place, it is a miracle of grace if he is able to look on his successor with friendliness and genuine good-will.

But in John this miracle was wrought. Not for an instant did he yield to the querulous suggestions of his followers; but with the utmost lucidity and serenity he set before them the logic of the situation. "A man can receive nothing," he told them, "except it be given him from heaven." That is to say, every one has his own gift and his own place; some must be first, and some second; there is nothing more disastrous or ridiculous than for the second, instead of filling his own place and doing his own work, to be pining for the place and the work of the first. He had been but as the star which heralds the lamp of day. "Christ," he said, "must increase, but I must decrease"—surely the most beautiful expression of humility ever uttered.

But John rose far above even this in the glowing image in which he set forth the relation between Christ and himself: "He that hath the bride is the bridegroom; but the friend of the bridegroom, who standeth and heareth him, rejoiceth greatly because of the bridegroom's voice; this my joy therefore is fulfilled." In Eastern countries the friend of the bridegroom corresponded to our groomsman; but his duties were much more comprehensive: not only had he to superintend the arrangements of the marriage, but he had even to act as intermediary in the wooing. John had been wooing the Jewish people, not for himself, but for Another; but, as the friend of the bridegroom, if he is a true man, rejoices when the bridegroom comes upon the scene and he can retire into the background, so he not merely did not murmur at the success of Christ, but greatly rejoiced in it, recognizing in it the very object for which he had been working all the time.

It was nobly said, and it was said from the heart; but how difficult it was to say we know from the difficulty of saying it after him. "He that hath the bride is the bridegroom"—the lucky man, the elect of Providence, wins the prize of fortune or fame, genius or beauty; but how hard it is, when we discover that the prize is not to be ours, to rejoice in his good fortune! Even in God's work it requires great grace to be glad that others have obtained greater gifts and better success; but it is a plain duty, and in fulfilling it John will be our teacher.

In this section of John's life we see two things closely united—testimony to Christ and humility of disposition. The conjunction is a natural and a happy one. He who is to bear witness to Christ must master his self-love. We cannot work for Christ's honor and for our own at the same time. Those who exhibit Christ to men must hide themselves behind him. On the other hand, nothing tends so much to produce lowly estimates of self as to have a high estitimate of Christ. Let him fill the eye and the heart, and we shall forget ourselves. What many of us need to silence our vanity and boastfulness is to have our mouth filled with the praise of the Son of God.

CHAPTER V.

THE ECLIPSE OF HIS FAITH.

Matthew 11 : 2-6; Luke 7 : 19-23.

The circumstances attending the incarceration of the Baptist will be more appropriately considered when we come to the tragedy of his death. In the meantime let it suffice to recall the fact that his work of reformation was suddenly and prematurely stopped by his being shut up in prison; and that there he had probably languished for months before we hear of him again.

Imprisonment was not, indeed, in the ancient world exactly the same thing as it is among us. A prisoner frequently enjoyed a great deal of freedom, and he could generally be visited by his friends, as is indicated in the parable which says, "I was in prison and ye came unto me." Hence the Baptist received information of what was taking place outside, and he was able to send messages to whomsoever he desired. One day he sent by two of his disciples to Jesus to ask, "Art thou he that should come? or look we for another?"

Learned men have taken strange offence at this narrative, as if it contradicted other parts of the Gospel. It is held to be totally irreconcilable with the testimony said to have been borne to Christ by the Baptist; because one who had received such divine tokens as were vouchsafed to John at the baptism of Jesus and had pointed out the Messiah so distinctly could never afterwards have asked such a question as is here attributed to him. But this is one of the instances in which learning overshoots itself, and the plain man or the simple Christian is wiser than his teachers. Those who are taught by experience are well aware that the soul has its fainting-fits, and that one whose faith at one time is so great as to remove mountains may at another time be weak and unbelieving. In the Gospel the Baptist is frequently compared with the prophet Elijah; and, if ever there was a man who was a giant in faith, it was Elijah; yet Elijah had his hour of weakness too. He who on Mount Carmel was able to stand up without flinching in the face of the prophets of Baal and the thousands of Israel was found on another occasion, in a pessimistic mood, far from the confines of the Holy Land, a fugitive from his work, and wishing only for himself that he might die. Even our Lord himself had his Gethsemane, when he prayed, "Father, if it be possible, let this cup pass from me."

In the hope of averting from John the reproach of being a doubter, some have supposed that it was not for his own sake but for the sake of his disciples that he sent the message. He never doubted, it is thought, but his disciples did; they clung too tenaciously to their own master and raised all kinds of objections to the Messiahship of Jesus. In order to convince them John sent them to Jesus himself, being confident that in his immediate neighborhood they would see things which would convince them and receive from the lips of Christ an answer which would be irresistible. But the reply of Jesus seems too directly addressed to John to admit of such an explanation.

Others have seen in John's question an utterance not of scepticism but of impatience. Jesus was too slow, John thought, and needed to be told what was expected of him. Hence, he sent him a broad hint that, if he was to make any impression on the popular mind, he must change his method and act in a way more characteristic of the Messiah. If this was John's thought he was not the only one of the friends of Jesus who took upon himself to administer such hints. Others also were disappointed with his slowness and attempted to hurry him. But Jesus always rejected such advice with indignation, and to offer it implied the most serious scepticism; for, if Jesus really was the Messiah, was he not far more capable than any adviser of knowing the times and the seasons?

It is not difficult to understand the causes which led to the obscuration of the Baptist's faith. He was a child of the desert, accustomed to free movement in the open air, and in a prison he was like a caged eagle. His reformatory work had been abruptly interrupted in full tide; and the impulses of enthusiasm and activity were rolled back cold upon his heart. Besides, Jesus was a Messiah very different from the one he had anticipated; John expected him to take to himself his great power and reign. Might it not, for example, have been taken for granted that the Messiah could not allow his own forerunner to languish in prison? If he were king, the Herods as well as the Romans would have to resign their power, and the victims of their jealousy and injustice would march out of confinement. But month after month passed and Jesus made no sign; it looked as if he had forgotten his friend.

The Baptist's scepticism was real, but it was honest; and we may learn from him how to manage our own doubts.

Observe three things.

First, he put his doubts into words. Doubt is most dangerous when it is vague; condense it into definite questions and immediately the light begins to break. Put it, for example, into John's questions: "Art thou he that should come, or do we look for another?" "He that should come"—how much faith is in that! When once the heart is persuaded that there is some one who should come—some one who must come because he is indispensable, to loose the bands of sin and to unite to God—it is not far from faith in Christ. For, put the other question, "Look we for another?" if Jesus of Nazareth be not the Man of men, where are we to look for him?

Secondly, John sent directly to Christ. He did not go on devouring his own heart in his cell; nor did he do what would have been worse, grumble to his disciples. Scepticism would be short-lived if we brought our doubts at once to God. He was a wise man who, in religious darkness, cried out, "Save me, O God, if there be a God."

Thirdly, John never thought of withdrawing his condemnation of the conduct of Herod and Herodias. Some have spoken of his doubt as treachery; but this is quite an exaggeration. It would have been treachery if, believing himself deceived and neglected, he had made this an excuse for renouncing his testimony and so obtaining release from prison. Never is religious doubt so dangerous as when it is made an excuse for giving the reins to the flesh. He who, though perplexed in faith, remains pure in deeds, will ultimately fight his way through doubt and come safely out on the other side.

Jesus did not go far for an answer to John's question. Apparently the Baptist's messengers came upon him in one of those moments of holy excitement when he was surrounded by a crowd of the diseased, whom he was healing, and by a still larger multitude of the common people, to whom he was preaching; and, pointing to the double crowd, the Saviour said, "Go your way and tell John what things ye have seen and heard: how that the blind see, the lame walk, the lepers are cleansed, the deaf hear, the dead are raised, to the poor the gospel is preached."

Apparently, in shaping this reply, he had in his mind the words of Isaiah: " Then the eyes of the blind shall be opened, and the ears of the deaf shall be unstopped: then shall the lame man leap as an hart and the tongue of the dumb sing." Thus had the evangelical prophet described the Messianic age; and here, Jesus hints, is the prophecy fulfilled to the letter.

This reply shows the importance attached by Jesus to his own miracles. In our day there is a tendency to slight the evidential value of miracles. It is frequently said we believe in the miracles because we believe in Christ, not in Christ because of his miracles. The warning was recently given by a person of eminence to the students of a theological seminary that, if they wished to win the present generation and attract cultivated minds, they must emphasize the ethical elements of Christianity, but keep the miraculous in the background. Now, there is a way of stopping the mouth of inquiry with miracle that is certain to repel thoughtful minds—as, for instance, when the Bible is first proved to be inspired and then the demand is made that everything contained in it be accepted without any attempt to comprehend it. If the Bible is from God then all it contains must be reasonable, because God is the Supreme Reason; and, therefore, the human reason should be invited to apply all its powers to the comprehension of the statements of the Bible. In the miracles attributed to the Saviour there is a divine reasonableness, and, therefore, they ought never to be presented to faith as mere wonders, but in their fine congruity with the character and the work of Christ. But to suppress the miraculous element in the gospel is not the way to win the world or to form a powerful Christianity. The image of Christ which has cast a spell over the human mind, and more and more is drawing all men to him, is one into which miracle enters. Some, indeed, at present, even in the Christian camp, are trying to persuade us that we may safely drop from our conception of Christ both his supernatural birth and his bodily resurrection. But this impaired and mutilated conception of Christ has been often weighed in the balance of experience and always found wanting. This is not "he that should come." The world requires a divine Saviour;

and that Jesus Christ is he is proved partly at least by his miracles, and especially by the miracle of his resurrection.

It may be remarked in passing that one of the most striking evidences in favor of the miracles of Jesus is found in the statement of one of the Gospels that "John did no miracle." Every theory of the miracles of Christ invented in the present century by unbelief amounts to this—that the age in which Christianity arose was a superstitious one, which almost unconsciously wove round remarkable personages a halo of miracle. Religious minds were especially influenced by the desire to place the leading figures of the Christian movement on a level with the foremost personages of the Old Testament; and, as miracles had been attributed to Moses and other prophets, so the feeding of thousands with a few loaves and the resurrection of dead persons appear as facts in the Christian records. The whole theory, however, breaks down in the case of the Baptist. If this myth-making tendency was so natural it is difficult to see why it should not have applied to him. Indeed, this would have been inevitable, because the idea pervades the Gospels that John was a new Elijah; and the Elijah of the Old Testament is a conspicuous miracle-worker. Why did not Christian tradition invent for John a cycle of wonders to bring him up to the level of his prototype? The very last reason for any statement in the Gospels which it occurs to scholarship of a certain type to think of is that the event recorded actually took place. Yet the Gospel, which records the miracles of

Jesus, says with simple veracity of his forerunner, "John did no miracle."

The proof which Jesus submitted of his own claims was an appeal to what he was doing. And this will always be the best evidence of Christianity—when it is able to point to what it can do. Christianity does not, indeed, now miraculously heal deafness, blindness, leprosy, and the like; but, as Jesus promised, it does greater things than these. By the diffusion of the spirit of philanthropy and by the use of scientific skill in the service of charity it not only heals all manner of diseases, but—what is far better—it is learning to prevent disease and to lengthen life on the large scale. It is making men and women new creatures: it is making the brutal wife-beater a tender husband, the drunkard a sober man, the harlot pure, the thief honest. It is transforming savage countries, which have been the abodes of horrid cruelty, into abodes of civilization, and changing the dregs of society into good citizens and members of churches. The scepticism of last century is usually supposed to have received its quietus through the publication of Paley's "Evidences" and Butler's "Analogy;" but it may be doubted if this be the correct reading of history. I should attribute the restoration of belief in at least an equal degree to the practical labors of Wesley and Whitefield. The church which saves most souls and does most to sweeten and purify domestic and political life is the church which is doing most to counterwork scepticism. The best evidence of Christianity is a converted man.

Jesus himself, in reply to the Baptist, laid special emphasis on the fact that he preached the Gospel to the poor, bringing in this after the mention of his miracles, as if it were the climax of the whole demonstration. And Christianity can never offer a more impressive evidence of divinity than when it is able to say, "To the poor the Gospel is preached." Over the entrance to the school of one of the greatest philosophers of Greece the legend was inscribed: "Let none ignorant of mathematics enter here." This was proof enough that not in philosophy lies the salvation of mankind, for the mass of our race will always be ignorant of mathematics. But by preaching to the poor Christianity shows that it is adapted to all, approaching men at that level where they are all alike and where are found their most cardinal wants; and it proves at the same time that it is animated with the spirit of Him who has made of one blood all nations of men to dwell on the face of all the earth, and who regards the humblest of his creatures with a Father's love.

To his message to the Baptist our Lord added what may be called a postscript; and, as the postscript of a letter sometimes contains the most important part of the whole communication, so Jesus sent to John one of the weightiest words he ever uttered, when he added, "And blessed is he whosoever shall not be offended in me."

It was a solemn warning, yet the wording of it was managed with consummate skill. Jesus might have said, "And cursed is he whosoever shall be offended

THE ECLIPSE OF HIS FAITH. 245

in me;" but that way of putting it might have inflamed a hot spirit like John's; so Jesus, with his perfect tact, put it the other way, yet in words fitted to excite in John's mind a fear of that which he had not expressed.

John was in a dangerous state of mind. If he had given way to his pessimistic mood he might have stumbled over the stone which he had been sent to lay in Zion as the chief corner-stone. His doubt might have ripened into denial; and he might have come to the conclusion that Jesus was not the Messiah. To prevent this, Jesus warned him not to give way to feeling, but to think: to think, that he who had already fulfilled so large a portion of the Messianic programme, sketched by Isaiah, might be trusted to fulfil the rest; to think, that it was not for him to prescribe the path of One whom he had acknowledged to be far greater than himself, but to leave it to his superior wisdom.

There was another danger to which John was exposed. He was a leader of men; he had many disciples, and his word carried weight with multitudes in every part of the country; if he had gone wrong, and declared against the claims of Christ, he would have led others astray besides himself, and his declaration could not but have been prejudicial to Christ's cause.

The question is sometimes raised, whether men are responsible for their opinions, and whether God will punish men for their unbelief if they have honestly been unable to believe in Christ. This is a much more difficult question than many think. It is easy to take for granted that doubt is honest. But in reality it may not be so. It may be a vague mist of opinion, in which the mind has allowed itself to become enveloped because it has never had the courage to think its doubts through. There may be vanity in it; for skepticism is sometimes worn as a feather in the cap. The claims of Christ are so great and have so much *primâ facie* authority that no one in a right state of mind can reject them without long labor and much pain. The responsibility of communicating doubt to others, that they may be withdrawn from the faith of Christ, is greater still; and those who feel that their duty lies that way may well beforehand ponder this word, "Blessed is he whosoever shall not be offended in me."

To a vast multitude in Christian lands, however, this word of Christ conveys a different message. They may have no intellectual doubts about Christ, believing him to be the Son of God and the Saviour of the world; but they are offended in him in another way. They are offended by his cross; they are afraid to confess him and to take the consequences. Their convictions about Christ are going one way and their conduct the other. Far oftener Christ addressed himself to this state of mind, and about it he expressed himself more plainly: "Whosoever shall confess me before men, him will I confess also before my Father which is in heaven; but whosoever shall deny me before men, him will I also deny before my Father which is in heaven."

CHAPTER VI.

HIS EULOGY.

Matthew 11:7-19; Luke 7:24-35.

It was as the messengers of the Baptist departed that "Jesus began to speak unto the multitudes concerning John." When people have departed, the language which breaks out behind their backs about them and their friends is too frequently of a questionable order. Gossip only waits till the door is shut behind a visitor before canvassing every defect in his appearance and ripping up the seams of his character. Those who have been all smiles and flattery to a person present will dissect with the most venomous relish the same person absent. But how different was Jesus, and what an example he has left in this as in other particulars! While John's messengers were present he was silent in his praise; indeed, he spoke rather in a tone of reproof. But no sooner were they out of earshot than he broke out in language of the warmest eulogy, as if his admiration had been pent up, and rushed forth as soon as it could find an outlet.

There are few things in biography more beautiful than the relations to one another of John and Jesus. John's trial took place when the multitude forsook him and went away to Jesus. Others envied for his sake; but not a thought of the kind could find its way into his heart; he only said, "He must increase, but I must decrease." The trial of Jesus, on the other hand, arrived when John sent his messengers to ask a depreciatory question. But He did not resent it. His language about John is full of generosity. There is in it even a poetic intensity, which shows from what a warm place in his heart it came.

Four things about John are embraced in Christ's panegyric: his personal character, his prophetic greatness, his success, and his failure.

The opening words—"What went ye out into the wilderness to see? A reed shaken with the wind? But what went ye out for to see? A man clothed in soft raiment? Behold, they that wear soft clothing are in kings' houses"—appear intended to protect John from the unfavorable impressions which may have been made by his own message. The question, "Art Thou He that should come, or do we look for another?" might have suggested in John a certain fickleness when contrasted with the emphasis of his earlier testimony; and it suggested an impatience which might be attributed to dissatisfaction with the hardships which he was enduring. Was John, then, a changeable mortal, sighing for release and comfort? From such a caricature Jesus lifted the minds of the listeners to the image of the real John as he appeared in the days of his prime. Was he, whom they went out into the wilderness to see, a reed shaken with the wind—one whom the wind of popular favor could sway this way or that, as it listed, or the stormy wind of persecution bend and break? Was he not, on the contrary, an Elijah-like figure—one fit to stand up against any odds and face the frowns of a hostile world? Was he a man clothed in soft raiment—one who loved his ease and shrank terrified from suffering? They could not but remember the emaciated figure and the coarse and scanty garb of the man of the desert. He had, indeed, had an opportunity of being a courtier, because Herod had cast on him a favoring eye and listened to his preaching with delight; but it was well known what use he had made of this opportunity—not in such a way as to be included among those who are gorgeously apparelled and live delicately in kings' courts, but in such a way as to doom himself to a dungeon.

Such was John—the uncompromising witness, able to stand like an iron pillar and a brazen wall against whosoever ventured to oppose the truth, the self-denying ascetic whom no threats could intimidate or sufferings tame—and Jesus loved to paint him in the glory of his prime. God always sees the best of his servants and places their character and their services in the most favorable light: not his the petty spirit which criticises everything that is high for the purpose of bringing it low, or judges a man by his worst hour rather than by his best.

It has been said that every man of prophetic endowment has to pass through the stages of criticism against which John was defended by Jesus. First, when he begins to attract attention, he is said to be a reed shaken with the wind: he is waiting for the popular breeze and will bend any way, as influence is brought to bear upon him. By and by, when he has conquered popularity, he is assailed with the second accusation—that he is a man clothed in soft raiment; he is making his friends among the rich and powerful, and is intent on feathering his own nest. Only after running the gauntlet of such criticism does he at last wring from the minds of his contemporaries the acknowledgment that he is a prophet. Perhaps this is true, and it is a lesson for the critics; but there is a solemn lesson for the man himself. Any one endowed with the prophetic gift will be tempted at precisely these points. He will be tempted first to use the gift of speech for the gratification of his own vanity, being puffed up or cast down according as the multitude follow him and the organs of public opinion praise him or not. Then, after his position is won and his fame established, he will be tempted to use his gifts to shape for himself a comfortable place in society. And only after he has surmounted both forms of temptation will he approve himself a true prophet of the Lord.

The Baptist, then, was no reed shaken with the wind or softly clothed courtier, but a true prophet. "Yea," the Lord added, "and more than a prophet; for this is he of whom it is written, Behold, I send my messenger before thy face, which shall prepare thy way before thee. Verily I say unto you, among them that are born of women there hath not risen a greater than John the Baptist; notwithstanding, he that is least in the kingdom of heaven is greater than he."

This is high and almost, one would think, excessive praise. Among those born of women, before the birth of Christ, must we regard John the Baptist as the very greatest man? Was he greater than Moses, Elijah, David, Isaiah; or—to glance beyond the elect people—greater than Homer and Plato, Sakya-muni and Confucius? Probably this was not what Jesus meant; and the difference in his meaning points to a profound difference between the human and the divine way of estimating greatness. We measure greatness by the size of the brain—by what we call brilliance, talent, genius. This flatters human vanity; and out of it arise the extravagances of hero-worship and the madnesses of ambition. But God's way of estimating greatness is different: greatness is to be sought in faithfulness to duty, in the humility with which the gifts of God are received and utilized; above all, in nearness to God himself. John was greater than all who had gone before him, not because the force of his manhood surpassed that of Moses, or because his prophetic style excelled that of Isaiah—for they did not—but because he was nearer to the divine Light which was coming into the world, and to him was vouchsafed the unique privilege of introducing it to mankind.

This explains the remarkable statement: "Notwithstanding, he that is least in the kingdom of heaven is greater than he." The comparison is not in reference to character or performance, but in reference to position and privilege. In a somewhat similar way we might say that a student of to-day is greater in mechanics than Archimedes or in astronomy than Copernicus; not in the sense that he has greater mechanical or astronomical genius, but in the sense that his position in time lifts him over the heads of those men of the past. John is regarded as still belonging to the Old Testament era, although so near the New Testament era as to be able to touch it and, therefore, greater than those more remote from it; but those in the New Testament era, even the least of them, are greater than he.

The New Testament era is here called "the kingdom of heaven;" and this suggests a comparison. We are accustomed to divide nature into three kingdoms—the mineral, the vegetable and the animal. Now, it can be said that what is least in the vegetable kingdom is greater than that which is greatest in the mineral kingdom, and that what is least in the animal kingdom is greater than that which is greatest in the vegetable kingdom. So he that is least in the kingdom of God, as Christ set it up in the world, is greater than he that was greatest in the imperfect dispensation of the Old Testament, just as he that was least there was greater than the greatest in the world which lay outside the sphere of revelation.

Such is the tenor of the whole New Testament. It will be remembered how St. Paul contrasts the ministration of condemnation, as he calls the Old Testament, with the ministration of the Spirit, as he calls the New Testament. The Old Testament was, indeed, glorious in comparison with the surrounding world; "but even that which was made glorious had no glory in this respect by reason of the glory that excelleth. For if that which is done away is glorious, much more that which remaineth is glorious."

We may well inquire wherein this glory or greatness consists; for, if we are Christians, it belongs to us. Everyone who is in Christ is greater than was Abraham or Moses, Isaiah or John the Baptist. This is not, indeed, a greatness of character, but of position and privilege; yet it is meant to react upon character. Indeed, this is the very spring of New Testament morality: it is the worldly maxim, *Noblesse oblige*, raised to a heavenly intensity. Ye are risen with Christ, therefore rise with him to newness of life; ye are seated with him in the heavenly places, wherefore set your affections on things above. This is the strain of the whole New Testament: it is from the sense of being ideally lifted up into a region of holiness and blessedness through our connection with Christ that we are supplied with the motive and the power for the real conflict with evil. "Ye are a chosen generation, a royal priesthood, a holy nation, a peculiar people; that ye should show forth the praises of him who hath called you out of darkness into his marvelous light."

From the Baptist's personal character and his official greatness the Lord goes on to speak of the success of his work: "From the days of John the Baptist until now the kingdom of heaven suffereth violence and the violent take it by force." These words are difficult; but not a few misinterpretations, which need not be mentioned, fall away when we observe that Jesus is still being carried forward on the tide of eulogy, and that these words, therefore, are words of praise, not of blame.

What John had done was to set the kingdom of

heaven in the midst, where it attracted the thoughts, the desires and the conversation of men. Through his eyes his hearers saw the kingdom of heaven as a city of which they must get possession, and, like resolute besiegers, not to be baulked, they were ready to do and to sacrifice everything in order to obtain this object of desire: "the violent take it by force."

The words, "The kingdom of heaven suffereth violence," would not mean anything more than is expressed by the second clause, "The violent take it by force." But perhaps a better translation would be, "cometh in with violence;" and this would naturally refer to the earnestness with which it was preached, whereas the other clause refers to the earnestness of the hearers. With this agrees the version of St. Luke: "The kingdom of heaven is preached, and every one presseth into it." John had not only been an earnest preacher himself, but he had raised up a race of preachers like-minded; and these earnest preachers made earnest hearers.

Whether in the words, "The violent take it by force," any reference is made to the character of John's converts is not certain. At any rate, his converts were the violent rather than the respectable. To the respectable Jesus said on a subsequent occasion, "John came unto you in the way of righteousness, and ye believed him not; but the publicans and harlots believed him." There was an element of violence in John's preaching; it was full of wrath and menace; it was not the pure or the full gospel. His hearers also were very imperfect; their previous lives had been violent and their apprehension of the kingdom of God was very defective; yet his was a genuine work, and it caused a genuine revival. Sometimes the preaching of the gospel may not be very refined; there may be too much terror in it, and it may lack the sweetness and light of mature Christianity. Yet, if it comes with power from the heart of the preacher, it may do infinitely more good than a perfect form of sound words preached without earnestness. Hearers awakened in open-air meetings or mission halls to flee from the wrath to come may press into the kingdom, while many who have heard the gospel for a lifetime in fashionable churches are dismissed into outer darkness.

Up to this point Jesus has proceeded in the strain of panegyric; here, however, comes a "but"—" But whereunto shall I liken this generation? It is like unto children sitting in the markets and calling unto their fellows, We have piped unto you and ye have not danced; we have mourned unto you and ye have not lamented."

Now a "but" after a panegyric is suspicious. In talking of others we sometimes say a certain amount of good, then suddenly, with a "but," the conversation takes a turn, and the good already spoken is undone by the envious and malignant sequel. The transition in the discourse of Jesus was not of this kind. He went on, indeed, to speak of John's failure to influence his generation as a whole; but his aim was not to depreciate John, but to attack those who had rejected him. And the final proof of the purity of his motive is that at this point he associates himself with John : the failure of the Baptist was also his own.

The language in which Jesus here speaks is very striking. It is figurative; and this is like him, for he loved to use similitudes. The imagery is taken from common life—the life of the street—and this also is characteristic. It is most characteristic of all that he borrows from the children's world; for of that world in all its phases he was lovingly observant.

Jesus had seen the children in the markets—as we may see them in our own streets—playing at funerals and marriages. One child would play the chief mourner, and the others would follow lamenting; one child would play the pipe, or something which could be feigned to be a pipe, and the rest would dance like the guests at a wedding. But soon the children tired, or something else attracted them, and the leader was left lamenting or piping in vain.

And there, said Jesus, are John and the Son of man. John came neither eating nor drinking: he was mournful, ascetic, funereal; and for a time it looked as if the whole country was to repent and mourn with him. But this seriousness did not last; the penitence of the people had not gone deep, and their impressions passed away. They threw the blame, however, on the preacher. "He is a little wrong in the mind," they said; "he hath a devil." Then came the Son of man, eating and drinking; and for a time his flute-like note of joy attracted more than had ever followed the mournful lead of the Baptist. But neither were the impressions permanent which He made; the enthusiasm cooled down, life returned to its ordinary channels, and they cast the blame on him. "A gluttonous man," they exclaimed, "and a winebibber, a friend of publicans and sinners."

These objections cancelled one another. Had it really been because John was too mournful that they left him they would have clung to Jesus, the joyful; had it really been because Jesus was too convivial that they left him they would have been satisfied with John. But their objections were merely excuses. The real reason was that they feared both John's glittering axe, "Repent," and the winnowing fan of Jesus, "If any man will come after me, let him deny himself." There are always excuses in plenty. One day it is too hot, another too cold; one church is too empty, another too full; one preacher is too learned, another not learned enough; one congregation is too genteel, another too common. But the real reason is still the old one—it is dislike to religion itself. Sinners do not wish to give up their sins, as John demanded; they do not wish to be brought nigh to God, as Jesus offered.

Such was our Lord's condemnation of his own generation; but it does not contradict what he had already said about John's success or deny entirely success to his own ministry. Though they had both failed with the generation as a whole, their mission was not wholly a failure; and this is what is expressed in our Lord's closing words: "But Wisdom is justified of her children." Those who slighted and rejected John and Jesus practically condemned the divine Wisdom which had sent these prophets; but there were those who condemned this condemnation and justified Wisdom. These were Wisdom's own children. In the preaching of John they recognized the accents of their lost mother, and they recognized them still more in the preaching of Jesus. But most of all did they discern the presence of divine wisdom in the combination of the two; because John's preaching of repentance awakened in them the sense of spiritual need, and in Christ's preaching the awakened soul obtained complete satisfaction.

In religion much depends on the preacher, and to his work is attached a heavy responsibility. But more depends on the hearer. Even when John' and Jesus were the preachers many hearers profited nothing. The preaching of repentance can do no good when sinners are determined not to give up their sins; and the unsearchable riches of the gospel are spread out in vain before those who are not hungering and thirsting after righteousness.

CHAPTER VII.

HIS MARTYRDOM.

Matthew 14:1-12; Mark 6:14-29; Luke 3:19, 20; 9:7-9.

We do not know for certain in what way the Baptist was got into the den of Herod. Den we may call it, because Jesus himself called Herod "that fox." Josephus says that the Baptist was imprisoned because the tetrarch feared that the crowds, attracted by his preaching might be used for revolutionary purposes. Most likely, however, this was only a pretext, and the gospels admit us to the real reason.

Probably John first obtained access to the palace in the way of his calling as a prophet. He was reaching all classes of the people, and he might well be gratified if anything opened the way to the highest circle of society; for a great preacher has a word for the highest as well as the lowest. Herod had a taste for preaching and probably invited the popular prophet to visit him. As the modern phrase would run, John was commanded to preach before the Court. And piquant must have been the contrast, as the son of the desert, dressed in his ascetic garb, trode the marble floors and appeared in the presence of those who were clothed in purple and fine linen.

A palace offers a pulpit which a preacher might envy. But it is a perilous place; it has chilled the message on many a preacher's lips, if it has not converted him into a flatterer and a sycophant. There have been shameful periods, in our own English annals, when the preachers of the Court have not only spared the sins of the great but profited by them, even bishops fawning for promotion at the heels of royal mistresses. On the other hand, when Court preachers have been true to their heavenly Master and dared to speak the truth even to royal ears, they have not infrequently had to risk not only position but life itself; and the Baptist is not the only one, by any means, who has thus lost his head.

Herod the Great—he who ordered the massacre of the babes of Bethlehem—left his dominions to be divided among four of his sons, each of whom was accordingly called a tetrarch; and Antipas—the Herod of the Baptist's life—thus became ruler of Galilee and Peræa. The father had been a man of the most unbridled passions, as well as of ability and magnificence, and his character was reproduced in this son; though the scope was much curtailed, he being a mere creature of the Roman masters of the country, by whose favor he was maintained in his place. It was the practice of petty rulers in his position to make frequent visits to Rome, where they danced attendance on the Court, waiting for any crumbs of imperial patronage which might come their way; and it was during one such visit to the Eternal City that Herod formed an intrigue with Herodias, the wife of one of his own brothers. It may be mentioned, as an indication of the disgusting state of morals which prevailed in the Herodian family, that both the husband whom this princess was quitting and the paramour whom she was following were her own uncles. Herod's intention was to divorce his lawful wife, when he reached home, and to marry Herodias; but, being informed beforehand of what was impending, his wife fled, before the approach of the guilty pair, to her father, Aretas, King of Arabia.

The relation of Herod and Herodias was, thus, of the grossest kind; and an honest preacher could not obtain access to the royal ear without stigmatizing so great a scandal. John did not go about the bush. Herod expected to hear the silken accents of oratory; but what he heard was a voice like the sound of a trumpet, saying without circumlocution, "It is not lawful for thee to have her." This was a sound unspeakably disconcerting, which it would never have done to allow inside the palace, and so John was cast into prison; the reason which Josephus gives being perhaps assigned as a pretext, because the real reason could not be avowed.

Although the tetrarch had shut John up in prison he was not, it would appear, incensed against him; for St. Mark's statement, that he "heard him gladly," appears to refer to the period of imprisonment. As the prisoner St. Paul had the privilege of preaching to Felix and Festus, Agrippa and Bernice, so, it would seem, John, though a prisoner, appeared before the Court and that again and again. Herod was a clever man; but his ability, being cramped in a position where he had little real power, ran to seed in a passion for novelty and excitement. The Baptist was an original; he was a man of mind, whose ideas were fresh; his appearance was striking and his delivery forcible; and the tetrarch derived from intercourse with him a welcome intellectual stimulation. Religion can be enjoyed in this way; it contains ideas, it is replete with mystery, and it can be preached with eloquence. A man may hear the word gladly, for the sake of the intellectual pleasure it affords and the interest of the preacher's personality, who has no thought of yielding to it his heart and his will. The same state of mind in Herod was exhibited at a later stage, when he was glad to see Jesus because he expected him to work a miracle. But by that time the star of his destiny was near its setting; and Jesus treated him with lofty disdain.

At this early stage, however, there was more in Herod than the insatiable curiosity of a man of pleasure. He feared John, we are told, " knowing that he was a just man and a holy." There was still a conscience in him. By one nod to a myrmidon to cut him down, when he uttered his uncourtly charge, he might have silenced the prophet; but he let him speak on; perhaps he even liked his faithfulness. Ungodly people sometimes admire a minister the more because he is not afraid of their faces and does not spare their sins. They know it is his duty; and they would despise him if he neglected it through fear of them. Policy is not likely to make a minister faithful, yet it is true that faithfulness is the best policy. And when faithfulness is backed up by character it commands the homage of all who are not utterly corrupt. As Herod listened he

HIS MARTYRDOM.

felt how awful goodness is, and his conscience consented to the law that it was good.

But conscience requires to be not only heard but obeyed; and this was where Herod lost himself, as multitudes do. He went further, indeed, than some. One version, apparently the better authenticated, says that he was much perplexed; another says, more significantly, that he did many things. Perhaps he prayed; perhaps he wept; perhaps he gave up this sin and that; perhaps he did this and that act of clemency or generosity. But one thing he would not do, and it was the one thing needful. All the time he was walking round this great thing in the centre of his life and the many things were only meant to make up for its omission. This is not an unusual position. There is one thing which people know must be done; they will multiply other things, they can do all other things, but this they will not and they cannot do. They hear God's thunder rolling overhead; they weep and pray; but still the one thing needful remains undone.

Meantime the conscience sadly suffers. Conscience ought to be obeyed instantly, and it is only by prompt obedience that its tone is maintained. But, if the condemning voice of the law is heard continually and assented to, but not obeyed, conscience becomes a mere pulp, in which nothing can take hold; the character is demoralized; and the indulgence of religious feeling and the multiplication of religious acts only make it worse. We can trace the history of the degeneration of Herod's conscience. When, some time after the Baptist's murder, the fame of Jesus reached his ears, he was still capable of an access of bewildering terror. "It is John the Baptist," he exclaimed, "risen from the dead." But, later, when the Baptist's Friend was sent to him for trial by Pilate, he had lost all dread and all shame; he behaved at first with the most cynical frivolty, and when the silence of Jesus dislodged him from this attitude he only made the transition to insane arrogance and mockery. His conscience had become seared. And this is the natural history of this faculty. Loyally followed, it is the surest guide to the heights of nobility and serenity, but tampered with, or neglected, it becomes the brand of moral degradation, while at the same time it hides within itself the secret of retributive torment.

The Baptist had no cause to apprehend immediate danger from Herod; but behind, the tetrarch there stood another figure, whose attitude was ominous. This was Herodias. What Jezebel was to Elijah in the Old Testament Herodias was to the Elijah of the New Testament. She was worse. Elijah escaped from the deadly hate of Jezebel and, as he had prophesied, her bones were devoured by the dogs of Jezreel; but John did not escape the vengeance of his enemy.

It has often been said that women are like the figs of Jeremiah: when good, they are very good, but, when bad, they are very bad.

> "For men at most differ as heaven and earth,
> But women, worst and best, as heaven and hell."

No symptom of the evil age in which the Messiah

came to this world was more noteworthy than the character of its women. The Agrippinas and Messalinas of Roman history, with their colossal passions, were the worst index of the ancient world's decay. And nowhere did this corruption assume worse forms than in Oriental courts, under Roman influence. In Cleopatra, the paramour of Antony, Shakespeare has depicted the type in all its features of mingled attractiveness and abandonment.

Herodias was a woman of this character. She had very good reasons for hating John; because, if Herod put her away, as John advised, where was she to go? For her the enjoyment and glory of life were over for ever. A woman's hatred is different from a man's. It sees its purpose straight before it, and no scruple is allowed to stand in its way. Herod, bad man as he was, feared John and reverenced him. Not so Herodias; for her there was no halo round the prophet's head. Either he must die or she be banished from the sunshine, a disgraced and ruined woman; and she did not hesitate a moment between the alternatives.

Josephus says that the Baptist was imprisoned in Machærus. This was a castle or palace in the neighborhood of the Dead Sea, that is, far in the south of the country; but Herod's regular abode was Tiberias, on the Sea of Galilee. It is just possible that Herod sent John to distant Machærus to be out of harm's way; for St. Mark says that "Herodias had a quarrel against him, and would have killed him, but Herod . . . . preserved him"; not "observed," as the common version says; the revised version renders, "kept him safe."

Even a prison may be a welcome protection from the wrath of an angry woman.

But Herodias' implacable hatred never slept, and at last her opportunity came. Herod was fond of all occasions which afforded an excuse for excitement; and he had borrowed from his Western masters the practice of celebrating his own birthday with elaborate festivities. Machærus was the palace chosen on this occasion, and there he assembled " the lords, high captains, and chief estates of Galilee." Herodias, too, was there. Herod, perhaps, had forgotten all about John, but she was thinking of nothing else.

The bait of which she made use was her own daughter. Few things in this world are more touching and beautiful than the training of a daughter by a good mother, whose cares and prayers fashion the virgin heart of her child into a sanctuary of all that is pure, modest and holy. But a wicked mother, transfusing into her daughter's heart the hellish passion and malignity of her own nature, is an awful spectacle.

Dancing is one of those things, innocent in themselves, which often serve the tempter as an inclined plane down which it is easy to get human beings to descend. Historically it has been associated with some scenes of the worst degradation of man and woman. In the corrupt age to which Herod belonged it was much sought after by men like him, and nowhere was it more relished than in Oriental courts. Both men and women practised it in public for a livelihood; and those who distinguished themselves were frequently rewarded by extravagant presents. Many of the dances were lewd in the extreme and appealed to the worst passions of human nature.

No doubt the favorable moment was watched for by Herodias, when the tetrarch and his boon companions had reached the stage at which evil passions can be most easily blown into flame. Then the girl was introduced, in her youth and beauty, and executed with bewildering grace the part for which she had been trained. The sight of one so nearly related to himself appearing in the position of a dancing-girl or play-actress ought to have filled Herod with shame and indignation; but the daredevil sauciness and the abandonment of a princess completely carried away the half-intoxicated men, who looked on spellbound and broke out into wild applause; and the tetrarch, entirely losing control of himself, roared out a promise to give her any present she might ask, even to the half of his kingdom.

One Evangelist says that the girl was instructed beforehand what to ask, while another says that she went to consult her mother. No wonder, however, that, even if she had been instructed beforehand, she went to ask when she received such an offer. Half of a kingdom! What might she not have obtained—palaces, jewels, gorgeous apparel—all that a girl's heart could desire! But that stony face, congealed with hatred and fear, met her hesitation unmoved. "Little fool, you know not what you ask: what would all these things be to you and me, unqueened and outcast, as we may be any day if John the Baptist lives?"

So she came back into the hall and said, "Give me here immediately the head of John the Baptist in a charger." She was still playing the saucy devil-may-care; and it is easy to imagine the roar of laughter and admiration with which the pretty wickedness of this request would be greeted by the tipsy revellers.

But Herod did not laugh. He grew pale and trembled; he knew that he had been entrapped. For a moment the fate of John and that of Herodias hung in the balance. Would the manhood and the kinghood in Herod prevail? Would he say, "No; I have been betrayed; no hand shall touch a hair of the head of the man whom I am protecting"? Alas, it was the opposite half of Herod's self which came forth—the weak, cowardly side. He was swept away by the drunken shouts of his courtiers; he affected to believe that he felt scrupulous about his oath. Perhaps the strongest motive of all was dread of the blood-thirsty Fury by whom the whole scene had been contrived.

Like mother, like daughter. Salome had played her part well. But what a burden was that for the girl to receive and carry away in the charger! Doubtless she kept up her gay and frivolous mood as long as the eyes of others were upon her; but surely her heart quailed when she was out of the lighted hall and alone with the ghastly object. The eyes of that other face, however, did not quail, but flashed with the fire of hell, as they devoured the hated features. When the head of Cicero was brought to Fulvia, the widow of Clodius and the wife of Antony, she drove her hair-pin again and again into the tongue which had denounced the iniquities of both her husbands; and Herodias was capable of doing as much at least.

She remained Herod's evil genius to the end. The death of the Baptist filled the tetrarch's subjects with horror ; and King Aretas led an army into the country to avenge the dishonor done to his daughter, inflicting on Herod a severe defeat which the people attributed to the wrath of heaven. Herod appealed to the Romans for help ; but in the nick of time the emperor died on whose favor he depended. Urged on by the ambition of Herodias he went to Rome, to pay homage to the new emperor and to beg for himself the title of king. But the new emperor, being prejudiced against him, not only refused his request but deprived him of his government altogether. Herod was banished to Lyons, in the south of France, where he and Herodias died miserably.

Nothing is told of the tragedy inside the prison. When the apparition of death confronted John so suddenly, how did he receive it? He was still young, little more than thirty ; the pulses of life were strong in him ; he had been arrested in the midst of a great work, and much, he must have felt, as every true worker for God and man feels, was yet to be done. Had he still a great doubt, which he was yearning to have solved before leaving the world?

There are few scenes more pathetic than the little company of his disciples gathering at the prison door to take up the poor, mutilated and dishonored trunk. Where did they bury it? It must surely have been in the sand of the desert—fit resting-place for one who had so loved solitude and to whom society had proved so unkind. Into his grave they dropped many a tear of affection; and many a golden hope and glorious dream they buried with their master. Were they thinking that surely Jesus, if he were the Christ, might have prevented this? Were they thinking of the enigma, that it should be possible for a man like Herod to put out of the world a man so good and so beneficent as John?

As they turned round from the grave, the heavens looked very blank and the earth very vacant. But a true instinct told them where to go—"They went and told Jesus." Ah, blessed road, whereon thousands upon thousands have followed them since! It is the right road, whatever be the trouble; but most of all when the waves and billows of doubt are breaking over the mind—when it looks as if Providence had let go the rudder, and as if there were no love at the heart of the universe. When the Son of God appears to have abandoned his own cause, and even to have given occasion to doubt his very existence, then carry the trouble to no one else, but go and tell Jesus.

> "God is his own interpreter
> And he will make it plain."

Long since has he made plain the martyrdom of the Baptist; for John has accomplished far more by dying than he could ever have done by living. He lives on in the world with an influence ever extending; it is even he who keeps alive the memory of Herod, Herodias and Salome, who murdered him. Whenever truth has to be defended or difficult testimony has to be borne, there his image sheds a welcome inspiration;

and because he gave up his life rather than compromise with sin, therefore his voice, crying, "Repent!" still echoes in the hearts of men, and his finger is visible across the centuries, outstretched towards "the Lamb of God, which taketh away the sin of the world."